ULTIMATEFIGHTER

Lockheed Martin F-35
Joint Strike Fighter

Bill Sweetman

ZENITH
PRESS

First published in 2004 by Zenith Press, an imprint of MBI Publishing Company, Galtier Plaza, Suite 200, 380 Jackson Street, St. Paul, MN 55101-3885 USA

Zenith Press titles are also available at discounts in bulk quantity for industrial or sales-promotional use. For details write to Special Sales Manager at Motorbooks International Wholesalers & Distributors, Galtier Plaza, Suite 200, 380 Jackson Street, St. Paul, MN 55101-3885 USA.

ISBN 0-7603-1792-5

Front and back cover, frontispiece, title page, and table of contents photos courtesy Lockheed Martin

Edited by Steve Gansen
Designed by Mandy Iverson

Printed in China

CONTENTS

CHAPTER 1

NOBODY PLANNED THIS

The sheer magnitude of the Lockheed Martin F-35 joint strike fighter (JSF) project is breathtaking. It envisages the production of 4,000-plus combat airplanes. If you are tempted to consider the JSF as a lightweight fighter, understand that the F-35 has more installed thrust than an F-4 Phantom and has a greater takeoff weight, bomb load, and range than a World War II B-17 Flying Fortress. Developing the new fighter will cost more than $40 billion; building 4,000 airplanes will cost well over $160 billion, even at today's prices.

If the program matches the longevity of the last new fighter to emerge from Fort Worth, the F-16 Fighting Falcon, the JSF will still be in production in 2035. Some F-16s are expected to serve for more than 35 years, so the last JSFs might not be retired until 2070. Taking inflation into account and looking at the high-end of production estimates, and adding 50 years of upgrade and support business, the notion of a trillion-dollar ($1,000 billion) project is not ludicrous.

The project's impact on the aerospace industry should be immense. Its aim is to replace most of the fighters in U.S. service, together with most of the modern fighters supplied by the U.S. to other air forces in the past 25 years. If it succeeds in this goal, it will starve most of the rest of the world's fighter projects of sales, and probably put their design teams out of business.

This in turn represents a major commitment of trust and resources to JSF, to Lockheed Martin, and to the United States government by customers and partners around the world. A fighter aircraft fleet today is a nation's most expensive and crucial military asset, with reach, firepower, accuracy, and flexibility that no other weapon system can match. Not only are partner nations relying on JSF to meet their key military needs, they are also aware that by participating in JSF they are part of a process that could eliminate most alternatives to the U.S. airplane by the early 2010s—before their JSFs have been delivered, before testing has been completed.

This outcome would be a tremendous achievement for an industrial strategy—had there been one. But the history of JSF is unique. The airplane's fundamental features were conceived by a community of dedicated outcasts who fought to sustain research into runway-free fighters in the face of complete indifference, and on occasion hostility from their major customers. The entire project was defined in three years in which the U.S. administration paid less attention to defense procurement than at any time since 1941. In late 1993, the acronym JSF had not been coined. Its precursor project, a limited technology demonstrator program, was not even funded. By the end of 1996, a single decision by the JSF program office wiped out two of the most illustrious names in aviation history.

Along the way, JSF has been sculpted by some remarkable individuals. A marine colonel and a test pilot with a Ph.D.; an air force general who took an experimental airplane, largely crewed by civilians, into battle in the first Gulf War; a bulldog-stubborn, pipe-chewing British engineer who never missed a chance to be undiplomatic. an entire crew of U.S. engineers whose determination to prove that they could build fighters was vital to the project, even though they did not win.

We can trace everything to the Wright Brothers if we want to, but the best starting point for the JSF story is Paris in the 1950s, when it was still cheap and romantic and smelt of Gauloises and, even more amazing, when France was part of the North Atlantic Treaty Organization (NATO).

The U.S. Army, itching to acquire its own air force, was the chief sponsor of jet VTOL developments in the United States in the early 1960s. Army funding supported General Electric's gas-driven lift-fan system tested on the Ryan XV-5A. Complex and vulnerable to damage, it was abandoned by the end of the decade. NASA

ABOVE: Five Royal Air Force Harrier GR.1 STOVL fighters in formation in late-1960s RAF camouflage. Statistically, two or three of the aircraft in this photo would have ended their careers in operational accidents. *British Aerospace*

RIGHT: A favored approach to VTOL in the United States, in the 1950s was the tail-sitter. The Ryan X-13 was the most successful of an indifferent bunch of airplanes and was demonstrated in the Pentagon parking lot, but the piloting difficulties were enormous. Bill Sweetman

U.S. Air Force Col. Willis Chapman had commanded a B-25 group in Italy from 1944 to 1945 (one of his bombardiers was an aspiring writer named Joseph Heller) and later headed the first USAF jet bomber group, flying B-45 Tornados. In 1956, he was sent to Paris as the USAF representative for the Pentagon's Mutual Weapons Development Plan (MWDP) field office. The objective of the MWDP was to find and support innovative ideas in Europe's defense industry—still recovering from wartime damage so it could make a stronger contribution to NATO's own defense.

Bill Chapman had not been in Paris very long when a French designer, Michel Wibault, approached his office with a design for a vertical take-off and landing (VTOL) fighter. It had a powerful turboprop engine connected by shafts and gears to four centrifugal "snail" fans on the sides of the fuselage. The fans could swivel through 90 degrees to point their exhausts downwards for take-off or aft for level flight.

Chapman was familiar with contemporary attempts to build VTOL fighters. Lockheed and Convair had built two extraordinary fighter prototypes for the U.S. Navy; fitted with enormous propellers, they stood on their tails for take-off and landing so that the pilot lay on his back with his feet in the air. ("A good position," Harrier designer John Fozard later commented, "but not for flying.") By 1956, the navy project had been cancelled, although Ryan was still working on the jet-powered X-13.

Other researchers were working on "flat-risers"—some with batteries of small jet engines that were used only for vertical lift, and others with swiveling engines, but the first involved carrying a great deal of dead weight in forward flight and the latter was mechanically complicated. Wibault's idea was different, Chapman thought, and worthy of further investigation.

The USAF officer showed the Wibault design to Dr. Stanley Hooker, technical director of the Bristol Aero Engine Company. MWDP had funded Bristol's Orpheus jet engine. Assigned by Hooker to look at the concept, engineer Gordon Lewis was impressed by Wibault's idea of deflecting the airflow and thrust, rather than rotating the airplane or the engine. Lewis designed a simpler engine which used the first two stages of Bristol's Olympus jet engine as a fixed, axial fan with rotating nozzles to deflect the exhaust. The idea

of using a shaft-driven fan to provide lift would not be revived for another 23 years.

A brochure on the resulting BE.53 engine reached Hawker Aircraft at Kingston in June 1957. Chief designer Sir Sydney Camm, whose Hurricane fighter had been the backbone of the RAF in the Battle of Britain, directed designer Ralph Hooper to explore its potential. Hooper saw that he needed all the vertical thrust the engine could provide in order to produce a workable aircraft. The BE.53 evolved into a turbofan with four rotating nozzles—one pair deflecting the fan stream and another for the core exhaust. When

Chapman visited the Hawker hospitality chalet at the Farnborough air show in September 1957, Hooper and Camm showed him a preliminary design for the P.1127, a small fighter with the BE.53 engine mounted at the mid-body position under a shoulder-mounted wing.

By May 1958, MWDP funding was paying for the BE.53 engine, now named Pegasus. Funding the P.1127 proved more difficult because the British Ministry of Defence (MoD) had little interest in fighters. In the previous year, the MoD's Defence White Paper had concluded that the English Electric Lightning short-range interceptor would be the RAF's last manned fighter of any kind. Hawker started building two prototypes on company funds, and the first aircraft was complete by the time the MoD agreed to support construction of six prototypes in August 1960. In the United States, NASA supported the program by building and testing small free-flight models. These demonstrated that, unlike most contemporary VTOL designs, the P.1127 could be flown without a complex autostabilisation system. On October 21, 1960, the first P.1127 made its first wobbly hovering flight.

Early tests demonstrated the fundamental advantage of what Hawker and Bristol were now calling "vectored thrust" over other VTOL concepts. The P.1127 had one engine, no thrust blockers, and no diverter valves. The engine's flow-path was constant from start to shutdown. Because the engine was fixed and the nozzles

LEFT: How about a nine-engine fighter? France's Mirage III-V with eight vertically-mounted, ultra-light lift engines from Rolls-Royce and a license-built Pratt & Whitney turbofan for cruise thrust was actually the first VTOL airplane to exceed Mach 2. Practicality was another matter. Dassault

ABOVE: Believing that the Harrier was not complicated enough, German's VFW-Fokker and partners built the VAK 191 with a "four-poster" Rolls-Royce RB.193 engine and two lift-jets, plus a tiny wing (it was designed for low-level strike) and internal weapon bay. EADS

LEFT: Hawker Siddeley's HS.1154 , a supersonic evolution of the Harrier with ramjet-type burners in its front nozzles, was intended as a Mach 2, multi-role fighter for the Royal Air Force and Navy. It reached the full-scale mock-up stage before being cancelled in 1964. BAe Systems

Germany's VJ101—developed by a consortium including Messerschmitt—owed some of its inspiration to 1950s work in the United States by Bell. Six small jet engines—four of them in two swiveling wingtip pods, two behind the cockpit—lifted the supersonic fighter off the ground. Any engine failure would have rolled the airplane instantly, leaving the pilot no way to escape. EADS

Russia's Yakovlev Yak-38 was designed in the 1960s as a shipboard fighter for the Red Banner Fleet, which had never had conventional aircraft carriers and went to sea in 1975 aboard the hybrid cruiser/carrier Kiev. Bill Sweetman

moved (courtesy of a Rube Goldberg arrangement of shafts and bicycle chains, energized by a compressed air motor), the thrust vector could be moved quickly and precisely. This, the designers and test pilots found, meant that the aircraft could combine jet and wing lift for a very short take-off. The take-off roll started with the nozzles aft for maximum acceleration. At about 60 knots, the pilot brought the nozzles to a 45 degree angle and the aircraft took-off.

With short take-off (STO), the P.1127 carried a much greater load than was possible in a vertical departure, and because of the low liftoff speed it needed only a few hundred feet of take-off roll. This was vital because—until that time—an airplane that carried enough thrust for a vertical take-off had little capacity for fuel or payload.

As prototype testing continued, the RAF prepared a draft operational requirement, OR345, for a V/STOL fighter based on the P.1127 design. Already, doubts about the wisdom of the 1957 no-fighters policy were beginning to spread.

At the same time, V/STOL was becoming the latest fashion within NATO, which was moving from the perilous "nuclear tripwire" strategy of the 1950s to "flexible response" strategy. Tactical air power would be vital in containing a non-nuclear Soviet attack, but long runways were obvious, fixed, and vulnerable targets for bombers and missiles.

In 1961, NATO basic military requirement 3 (NBMR-3) defined a joint specification for a supersonic V/STOL fighter-bomber. Its importance was symbolic, since there was no commitment from any NATO country to buy the winning aircraft, but it spurred the RAF to drop OR345 in favor of the more ambitious NATO concept.

Hawker designed the P.1154, a hulking beast with a 33,000-pound-thrust Bristol Siddeley BS.100 engine. It was one of the most powerful jet engines ever designed, with ramjet-like afterburners on the swiveling front nozzles. Hawker built a full-scale mock-up at Kingston, and work went forward on the fighter and an array of advanced systems: a Ferranti multi-mode radar with air-to-air and terrain-following capabilities, one of the first head-up displays, and an inertial navigation system.

Companies in France, Germany, the Netherlands, and Italy proposed radical supersonic V/STOL fighters. The first two were the most serious contenders. Dassault, working with Rolls-Royce, modified one of its Mirage prototypes with no fewer than nine engines: one to propel the airplane in flight and eight small vertical jets for take-off and landing. A German consortium, EWR, flew the VJ 101, with four engines paired in swiveling wingtip nacelles and two lift-jets behind the cockpit. The Netherlands' Fokker D.24 Alliance, supported by Republic Aircraft, combined the BS.100 engine with the then-fashionable variable-sweep wing.

Hawker and Bristol's P.1154 was declared the technical winner of NBMR-3, but no NATO member put any money into it except for Britain, which selected it to replace the RAF's Hunters and the Royal Navy's Sea Vixen all-weather fighters. (In early 1963, one of the P.1127s became the first jet V/STOL aircraft to land on an aircraft carrier.)

Definition did not proceed smoothly. The RN wanted a twin-engine aircraft, so Hawker designed a P.1154 with two Rolls-Royce Speys. It had a complicated cross-ducting system so it would not turn upside-down if one engine failed in jet-borne flight. The RN wanted a larger radar and a two-man crew. In fact, what the Navy wanted was an F-4 Phantom; this is what the RN received after the P.1154 was cancelled in early 1965. Britain's new socialist government, blissfully free of any technological and industrial knowledge, was determined to cut the country's defense expenditures.

John Fozard, a forthright engineer and one of Camm's disciples, played an increasingly important role in the V/STOL project. He later reflected that "we'd probably have made the 1154 work, but we'd have learned to live with operational restrictions." Already, two V/STOL design issues were being recognized as more than just nuisances.

One of these was the effect of jet blast on the landing surface. On one of the first P.1127 hover tests, it was discovered that the jet exhaust hit the ground and spread out radically as a thin sheet of fast-moving air. Speed results in less air pressure at the surface and, as the test team found out, it takes a relatively modest pressure differential to turn a manhole cover into a hostile UFO. But the faster, much hotter blast from the P.1154's front nozzles would have been more destructive, blasting loose dirt in all directions, softening and destroying asphalt.

The other problem was hot gas re-ingestion, or HGR. Jet engines produce less thrust as outside temperature increases; the hotter the air entering the engine, the hotter the air inside it, so limit temperatures are reached at lower throttle settings. A V/STOL aircraft descends into a cloud of hot gas from its exhausts, with its inlets sucking air from all directions.

Fortunately, Hawker's eggs were not all in one basket. While the P.1154 was being designed, the United Kingdom, United States, and West Germany had funded nine improved P.1127s, named Kestrel. The initial U.S. support came from the army, which had felt since Korea that the

U.S. Air Force had no interest in the messy and dangerous business of close air support. The army was quietly attempting to acquire its own jets.

When the P.1154 was canceled, the U.K. MoD ordered an operational version of the Kestrel, the P.1127 (RAF), named the Harrier. It entered service in 1969, by which time almost every other V/STOL development in the world had fizzled out. The U.S. Army had sponsored two V/STOL designs: the Lockheed's XV-4A Hummingbird that couldn't lift its own weight off the runway, and the Ryan XV-5A—designed by General Electric and fitted with big fans in the wing, driven by engine exhaust—that proved unreliable. The two prototypes were involved in two fatal accidents. (General Electric adapted the technology into what it first called the "cruise fan"—it was the ancestor of today's high-bypass turbofan engines.) In any event, the U.S. Army had lost its roles-and-missions fight with the USAF and had been put out of the jet business.

Dassault's Balzac VTOL demonstrator suffered one fatal accident, was rebuilt,

The appearance of the Kiev helped secure support for the United Kingdom's shipboard version of the Harrier, to be flown from the relatively small Invincible-class helicopter cruisers. The Sea Harrier FRS.1 was a minimum-cost adaptation of the basic design with a slightly improved cockpit and a nose-mounted radar. BAe Systems

LEFT: In the Falklands War of 1982, RN Sea Harriers and RAF Harriers operated side-by-side from the Navy's Invincible and Hermes. Operations were patchy and marred by accidents, but the Harriers provided a vital level of protection against Argentine aircraft. U.K. MoD

and crashed again; the bigger, operational-size Mirage III-V became the first (and so far only, 38 years later) VTOL airplane to exceed Mach 2, in September 1966, but the project was one of many abandoned due to a creaking economy. In 1969, apart from the Harrier, the only surviving Western jet V/STOL program was Germany's VAK 191, a tiny-winged monster that combined a Harrier-type vectored thrust engine with two lift engines and consumed Deutschmarks and fuel at a great rate to little effect.

Apart from the RAF, the only full-scale V/STOL program belonged to the Soviet Navy, which had been prevented from building aircraft carriers in the 1950s when Khrushchev axed most of Stalin's shipbuilding program. The Red Banner Fleet was trying to gain a small fixed-wing capability using hybrid carrier-cruisers and V/STOL fighters. An awkward little prototype, the Yakovlev Yak-36, appeared at an air show in Moscow in June 1967; nine years later, when the carrier Kiev made its first sortie into the Mediterranean, operational Yak-38 V/STOL fighters lined the deck.

By 1970, though, the Harrier was the only V/STOL fighter in production, and soon became unique in another way—the only foreign fighter to be acquired by the United States

Tiny compared to U.S. supercarriers, Invincible and Hermes sustained operations in appalling weather. The plan was to establish an expeditionary airstrip on the Falklands for the RAF Harriers, but the materials were lost when the freighter Atlantic Conveyor was sunk. U.K. MoD

Rockwell International issued glossy brochures showing how the jet-augmentor flaps of the XFV-12A supersonic STOVL demonstrator would give it excellent maneuverability in combat. That might have been the case had the airplane been able to fly in the first place, which it could not. Boeing

in peacetime. The U.S. Marine Corps first evaluated the Harrier in 1968. With remarkable speed, the marines secured approval to buy 110 AV-8A Harriers, and an order was signed in 1970.

The marines wanted the Harrier because marine aviation had a unique mission. Far more than any other air arm, it was dedicated to close air support (CAS), attacking targets that were in direct contact with troops on the ground. The marines had pioneered CAS before World War II, primarily because (unlike other ground forces) they had no heavy artillery. During World War II, the Allies used fighters—Tempests and Mustangs—for CAS, but as post-war air forces switched first to jets and then to supersonic fighters,

CAS fell by the wayside. Supersonic fighters were too fast for visually aimed strikes against fleeting targets.

The marines were determined to retain their own air-power, independent of the navy's carriers, for one reason: Guadalcanal. In August 1942, 11,000 marines landed on the Japanese-held island. The day after the landing, Rear-Admiral Jack Fletcher, in command of the supporting aircraft carriers, pulled his ships back to protect them from air attack, forcing the withdrawal of transports carrying reinforcements and supplies. Forty-five years later, a marine at a V/STOL conference could still complain that "when the going gets tough, the carrier disappears over the horizon, we've known that since Guadalcanal."

In the 1970s, neither the United States nor the United Kingdom would fund development of a new engine for the Harrier. McDonnell Douglas, instead, designed a more efficient, light-weight wing made of carbon fiber composite with flaps and other devices to boost the airplane's lift. It was tested on the YAV-8B, seen here (top) in formation with a NASA AV-8A. NASA

At Guadalcanal, the marines got air cover once they had hacked Henderson Field out of the jungle. Jets required more support. The Marine Corps entered the jet age with the small, agile A-4 Skyhawk, and even developed a land-based, portable airfield, complete with catapult and arresting gear, so the fighters could move ashore with the troops. The Harrier was about as fast as the A-4, and about the same size, and made it possible to dispense with that cumbersome piece of equipment. Better yet, it could take off from navy "amphibs"—the big flat-deck amphibious-warfare ships which transported marine brigades into action.

The early history of the Harrier laid the foundation for what became JSF. From its conception, the V/STOL fighter was a product of Anglo-American collaboration, including the early MWDP backing for the engine and the army's support for the Kestrel. The USMC would become the largest and most dedicated operator of the Harrier, and would play a pivotal role in its development.

V/STOL acquired another institutional supporter in 1975. The Royal Navy (RN) had turned up its nose at the P.1154 in favor of F-4s; but before they arrived, its new carrier project

The final version of the U.S.-U.K. Harrier II was the AV-8B Plus, fitted with a Raytheon APG-65 radar in the nose and an infra-red camera above the radome. During the 1990s, most of the marines' surviving Harriers were modified into this configuration. Boeing

After the Falklands, it was recognized that the Royal Navy's Harriers needed a longer-range radar and missile to defend the fleet. The FRS.1 Harriers were re-worked into FA.2s, with the Ferranti Blue Vixen radar and AIM-120 AMRAAM missiles.
BAe Systems

had been cancelled. When the navy's aging carriers were paid off by the late 1970s, the service would have no replacement. However, the RN had been permitted to build three cruisers with full-length flight decks. Nominally built to carry large anti-submarine helicopters, the new ships were designed with V/STOL in mind. The U.K. MoD approved development of the Sea Harrier FRS.1 in 1975.

The Harrier was an impressive achievement, but had some inherent limitations. It was subsonic and had a short range. The RAF and marine aircraft carried no radar, so their air combat capability was limited. (The Sea Harrier had a small radar.) The Harrier also had a mean streak. Unusually, the P.1127, Kestrel, and Harrier made their way through flight tests until 1968 without a single fatal accident, but the statistics started to change as service pilots faced the challenge of flying the new jet.

In "up-and-away" flight with the nozzles pointed back, the Harrier flew like any other jet fighter. Short take-off was fairly straightforward: by the time the fighter left the ground, it was going fast enough for the aerodynamic controls to be effective, and the Pegasus engine provided brisk acceleration into a normal flight regime.

Landing was another matter.

As the airplane slowed down, the functions of the flight controls changed. The pilot had to use four controls—stick, rudder, throttle, and nozzle-angle control—to manage the aircraft. The stick and rudder were connected to both the conventional controls, which became useless as the airplane slowed down, and "puffers" in the nose, tail, and wingtips, jet-reaction controls driven by hot air from the engine, which worked at low speeds and in the hover. But the puffers were not the same as regular controls. They

A Marine Corps AV-8B lands vertically. Debris is always a problem in off-runway operations, even with the relatively low-velocity Harrier exhaust. Boeing

By the early 1980s it was clear that a high-powered "three-poster" STOVL fighter, with augmentors on the front nozzle, would have to be laid out to keep the structure out of the way of the jet blast. One result was the British Aerospace P.1216 design, with the tails and weapon racks carried on twin tailbooms. BAe Systems

changed the airplane's attitude, not its flight-path. With the nozzles down, changes to the airplane's attitude also changed the direction of thrust. Forward stick, for example, tipped the airplane forward and rotated the thrust vector aft, so the airplane started to move forward. Side-to-side stick movements would make the Harrier translate sideways. All the controls were mechanical and all of them were independent.

As one experienced Harrier pilots puts it: "The nozzle lever means there are two things for the left hand to grab, so it is only a matter of time before you move the wrong one. However, 40-plus years ago there was just no other way to do it. Generations of pilots have been trained up to the task and compensated for the deficiencies in the basic design concept, most of the time."

Experienced test pilots could make the Harrier spin on its axis, move forward, backward, and sideways, and—their favorite air show trick—drop a curtsy to the VIP enclosure. Lesser mortals knew that getting on the ground safely was accomplishment enough. If the aircraft started

to change speed or attitude too quickly, and particularly if it started to sideslip—the nose yawing to left or right at low speed—it could rapidly roll out of control, often into a position where ejection was impossible. "If I yell 'Eject!' and you say 'Pardon?'," one test pilot told a VIP before a demonstration flight in a two-seat Harrier, "you'll be talking to yourself."

After six years of training and operations, the RAF had taken delivery of its first 92 Harriers and had lost 18 of them in accidents. Of the 140-plus first-generation Harriers delivered to the RAF, 62 of them crashed. Many of the accidents were unrelated to V/STOL; the Harriers were used for low-level offensive support missions and had their share of bird-strikes, mid-air collisions, and ground impacts, but the overall record is one of the worst for any airplane. The marines had a similar experience, losing 42 of their 110 first-generation Harriers.

The accident rate received little publicity. RAF accident statistics, through most of the 1970s, were an official secret; accidents themselves were reported only to local media. The U.S. media's general indifference to the military kept the USMC rate under cover until December 2002, when the *Los Angeles Times* made the story the center of a Pulitzer-winning investigation. But service insiders were all too well aware of the problem, fostering a hardening prejudice against V/STOL.

As the USMC introduced the Harrier, the U.S. Navy commenced a flirtation with V/STOL. When Admiral Elmo Zumwalt became Chief of Naval Operations in 1970, the navy had a problem: its World War II-era *Midway* and *Essex*-class carriers were approaching retirement, and there was not enough money to replace them with supercarriers like the new *Nimtiz*. The *Nimitz* itself would not be commissioned until 1975 and only one more ship was

planned for the decade. Zumwalt ordered a study of alternatives that resulted in a Sea Control Ship, designed for convoy defense and equipped with supersonic V/STOL fighters and ASW aircraft.

In 1971, the navy invited manufacturers to propose demonstration programs for the new aircraft, and this was inundated with ideas. Lockheed-California proposed a propeller-driven tail-sitter. Boeing and Northrop designed jet tail-sitters. British Aerospace (BAe), formed in 1974 by the nationalization and merger of Hawker Siddeley and British Aircraft Corporation,

Veteran Harrier designer Ralph Hooper holds a model of the P.1216. Its biggest problem, in the early 1980s, was political: the MoD and RAF were determined to collaborate with Germany on development of a new fighter— only because it would make the project almost impossible to cancel—and Germany was not buying any form of STOVL. BAe Systems

McDonnell Douglas used NASA funds to carry out studies and wind-tunnel tests of a number of Model 279 configurations, all based to some extent on PCB Harrier-type concepts. This version had a canard layout. NASA

The Shoeburyness tests showed that most of the problems of PCB could be handled. However, it still caused problems with ground erosion and the side-mounted nozzles were incompatible with stealth, and PCB-Harrier studies had been abandoned by the end if the 1980s.

teamed with McDonnell Douglas to propose both an improved subsonic Harrier and a supersonic version with PCB.

The navy chose Rockwell to build the XFV-12A. For take-off and landing, the exhaust from the XFV-12A's engine was ducted to "augmentor" flaps in the wings and in the over-sized canard. By dragging free-stream air through the flaps and increasing the mass flow, the augmentor flaps would boost the engine's thrust by 70 percent, in theory, but not in practice. John Fozard could not resist pointing out that the P.1127, in its first tests, had been tethered down, while the only way that the XFV-12A's propulsion could be tested in free flight was to lift part of its weight with a crane.

The Rockwell fighter's performance, or its lack thereof, was academic. The Navy's nuclear and aviation communities detested the SCS, and in the 1974 budget debate, their friends on Capitol Hill scuttled it. (The "nukes" and the avi-ators recognized their debt to the chairman of the Senate Armed Services Committee, which is why the seventh *Nimitz*-class carrier is named the *John C. Stennis*.) Zumwalt was defeated, and the experience inoculated the USN against V/STOL—henceforth, anyone proposing a

V/STOL fighter for the USN was assumed to be a supporter of small, flimsy carriers.

After the navy rejected the Harrier developments, BAe and McDonnell Douglas tried to interest the U.S. and British governments in the powerful subsonic aircraft. Neither would fund it, but the U.S. Marine Corps sponsored a demonstration program, led by Douglas, which aimed at increasing the Harrier's range and payload at minimum cost. A new wing and other changes were tested on the YAV-8B, a modified AV-8A, starting in 1979. The USMC decided to replace all its AV-8As and A-4 light attack aircraft with a production version, the AV-8B Harrier II.

The Royal Air Force was still undecided about V/STOL in the late 1970s. Some factions in the RAF looked at the Harrier's subsonic speed, its accident rate, and the genuine logistical difficulties involved in off-base operations, and as a result wondered if the service should concentrate on conventional take-off and landing (CTOL) fighters. On the other hand, there was concern about the survivability of conventional air bases; the RAF itself was working on an airfield attack weapon that combined concrete-breaker bombs with mines that would destroy repair vehicles.

By this time, a change had entered the U.K. vocabulary. The term V/STOL gave way to STOVL (short take-off, vertical landing). The change recognized the fact that Harriers in service invariably operated in STOVL mode, using 1,000 to 1,500 feet of road, taxiway, or other level surface to take off.

In 1976, the MoD issued air staff target (AST) 403, calling for an agile fighter with a good ground-attack capability. BAe's two fighter divisions both produced designs to AST 403. The ex-Hawker Kingston group produced the P.1205,

ABOVE: One important British trial series in the 1980s involved this outwardly standard T.2 two-seat Harrier. The forward cockpit controls were linked to a sophisticated fly-by-wire system which allowed the airplane to be flown without a separate nozzle-angle control. Lessons learned on this program were carried over to JSF. BAe Systems

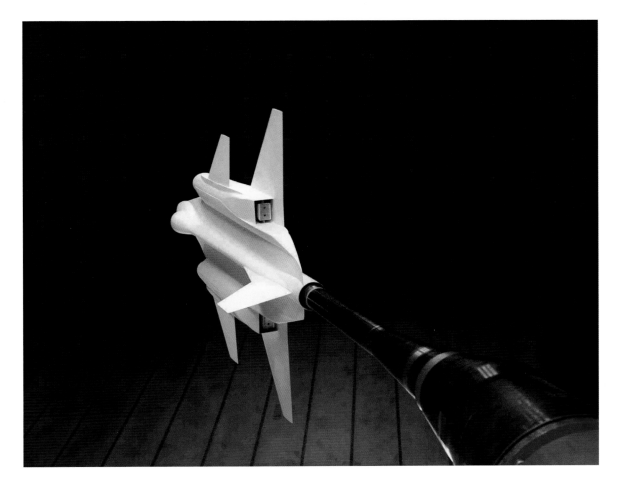

NASA and U.S. industry explored a number of STOL and STOVL concepts after the XFV-12A flopped and the Navy dropped its plans for V/STOL carriers. This jet-deflection STOL fighter was studied by General Dynamics. NASA

A NASA-sponsored study produced this wind-tunnel model. The large inlets suggest that it is a Harrier-type airplane with retractable vectoring nozzles. NASA

with West Germany, and the Luftwaffe hated STOVL as much as the U.S. Navy did.

The U.K. MoD consequently split its fighter requirement in early 1979. AST 403 was a CTOL multinational aircraft, and eventually led to the EuroFighter Typhoon. Air Staff Requirement (ASR) 409 was written around an improved Harrier; although Kingston proposed its own big-wing Harrier design, the MoD elected to join forces with McDonnell Douglas on the U.S. version.

The United Kingdom's domestic STOVL efforts suffered another blow in that year, when the British government announced plans to dispose of the RN's light aircraft carriers and Sea Harriers. But in April 1982, before these could be put into effect, Argentina seized the Falkland Islands.

To the Argentines' surprise, the British dispatched a task force to retake the islands, including the carriers *Invincible* and *Hermes* and 28 Sea Harriers. The Sea Harriers proved essential in blunting Argentine air attacks, shooting down 31 Argentine aircraft with no combat losses.

Ten RAF Harrier GR.3s were assigned to the force, but their departure was delayed by training to deliver laser-guided bombs and modifications, which allowed them to carry AIM-9 missiles. The first six aircraft were flown to Ascension Island, where they flew to the containership *Atlantic Conveyor* and landed on its deck. The ship followed the task force to the Falklands, where the Harriers flew to *Invincible* and *Hermes* before the containership was attacked and sunk. The last four RAF Harriers to join the task force launched from Ascension, and with the help of Victor tankers, flew 4,000 miles into the South Atlantic, where, on a pitching deck in a war zone, their pilots made their first carrier landings.

Nine aircraft were lost in the campaign. Three of the RAF aircraft and two Sea Harriers were lost to ground-fire. Early in the operation two Sea Harriers vanished in severe weather, probably as a result of a mid-air collision on patrol. One Sea Harrier slid off a carrier's deck while taking off in a Force 6 gale, and another crashed into the sea on take-off.

Operations were carried out in weather that ranged from poor to appalling. There were four basic weather states, which became defined as: fog, with 30kt winds; clear weather, with 30kt winds; gale conditions; and good weather, defined as sea state four or better. Conventional

blending some distinctly F-16-like features with a four-nozzle PCB engine.

In terms of performance, both aircraft were comparable, but politically, P.1205 was a non-starter. The cancellation of key projects in the mid-1960s traumatized the RAF. The only reason the Labour government of the 1970s did not axe the RAF's only new warplane, the *Panavia Tornado*, was that it was a multinational program and could not be scrapped without wrecking U.K.-German relations. Any new fighter would be multi-national. Realistically, this meant working

carrier-based aircraft cannot normally operate when the deck is pitching more than six or seven degrees, but the sea state did not affect Harrier operations at all, thanks to vertical landing. The Harriers landed opposite the island, where the pitching movement was smallest.

Fog did affect operations, and the aircraft sometimes had to find the carrier by its lights. One Sea Harrier was caught in fog and found the carrier on its second attempt with only 200 pounds of fuel left. The fog was so thick that the deck crew never knew the Harrier had landed.

Reports of the Harrier's success soon reached Washington, and some people began to ask the U.S. Navy where its V/STOL plans had gone. Navy Secretary John Lehman retorted that the U.S. Navy would have been protected from air attack by its supercarriers and F-14s. He

was right to a point, but at the time he did not know something. At times in the Falklands, Sea Harriers flew when the cloud-base was less than 100 feet above the ocean and horizontal visibility was barely 250 yards, or the distance from *Hermes'* stern to her bow. Absolute minima for U.S. Navy operations are 200 feet ceiling and 880 yards visibility.

By late 1982, the multinational Harrier program was healthy. More than 400 AV-8Bs, GR.5s, and Sea Harriers were on order. The RN's carriers had been reprieved. The USMC and RN were firmly committed to STOVL as the long-term solution to their air power requirements. The Spanish Navy had adopted the AV-8A in the mid-1970s India acquired Sea Harriers in the mid-1980s, and Italy was building a new STOVL-capable carrier.

Ejector lift augmentation—in which a high-speed airflow drags ambient air through a duct, theoretically boosting low-speed thrust—failed dismally on the Lockheed XV-4 in the 1960s and on the XFV-12 in the 1970s, but that didn't stop NASA and General Dynamics from trying in the 1980s with this design, seen in the form of a near-full-scale powered model. Third time was not the charm. NASA

Ultimately, all these aircraft needed replacement, and it was this requirement that kept a flickering flame underneath the pot of advanced STOVL technology during most of the 1980s. Flickering, because the environment for STOVL was otherwise inhospitable.

Anyone mentioning STOVL within earshot of the big-deck U.S. Navy was keel-hauled. The RAF was increasingly focused on EuroFighter. The U.S. Air Force, with most of the world's research money, was more interested in stealth than STOVL. The service was concerned about the danger posed by anti-runway weapons, but it was convinced that STOL was the best compromise. The replacement for the F-15, the new advanced tactical fighter, was to have thrust reversers that could operate in flight, allowing it to use 1,500-foot runways. (The reverser system was tested in flight on a modified F-15 and found to be heavy and complex, and STOL was dropped from the ATF requirement before the prototypes flew.)

It fell to pure research organizations to keep STOVL moving. In the United States, the center of this work was NASA's Ames Research Center at Moffett Field on the edge of San Francisco Bay. The immense 40x80 foot low-speed wind tunnel at Ames was ideal for research into STOVL and other projects that NASA grouped under the heading of "powered lift," and Ames was also a leader in the new art of computational fluid dynamics (CFD), the use of supercomputers to model and predict aerodynamic performance. In the United Kingdom, the Royal Aeronautical Establishment, later known as the Defence Research Agency (DRA), and now part of the Defence Engineering Research Agency (DERA), retained a strong interest in STOVL at its research sites at Farnborough and Bedford.

As members of a heretic minority, the British and American STOVL communities forged strong professional bonds, staging a biennial Powered Lift Conference that alternated between U.K. and U.S. locations. Since the high sheriffs in London and Washington regarded STOVL as unimportant, information flowed quite freely.

Between 1980 and 1985, NASA sponsored wind-tunnel work and theoretical studies on several STOVL concepts that

Intended follow-on to the Yak-36 was the Yak-141, with a single afterburning turbofan engine plus two lift engines. Supersonic and fitted with a radar, it was intended to be a multi-purpose fighter for a new generation of Russian carriers. Bill Sweetman

RIGHT: Lockheed and Rolls-Royce, in the late 1980s, studied a "tandem-fan" supersonic STOVL concept with a variable-cycle engine. It was the starting point for the shaft-driven lift-fan concept, which accomplishes much the same job with less complexity. Lockheed Martin

had fallen out of the U.S. Navy's ill-fated supersonic V/STOL escapade. Broadly speaking, the U.S. Navy requirements from the 1970s were used as a yardstick to compare the different concepts.

In the United Kingdom, BAe's Warton design team built a full-scale mock-up of an ultra-STOL fighter with twin tilting engines, the P.103, and Kingston continued to work on PCB designs, building a mock-up of the twin-boom P.1216.

A great deal of basic research was performed on problems such as flight control and the complex interaction between the hot exhaust gases, the ground, and the airplane. The advent of fly-by-wire flight controls, reliable inertial sensors, and digital engine controls could make it easier to control a jet-lift airplane, but the sheer thrust involved in a supersonic design could make it more difficult.

Aircraft-to-ground interactions were another good-news-and-bad-news story: new jet engines offered much more thrust per pound of weight than the Harrier's Pegasus, but the inevitable corollary was a hotter, faster exhaust that

could buckle decks, soften and rip concrete, damage unprotected ears, and turn any loose object into a missile.

As this work continued, U.S. and U.K. leaders quietly worked to set up a formal joint program. At a Farnborough conference in June 1983, four promising STOVL systems were identified as candidates for joint exploration. All were single-engine types and could be ready for service entry by 2000-2010, when the Harrier II would need replacement. In discussions with the USMC, RAF, and RN, a basic set of operational requirements was defined, allowing a fair comparison between the different concepts. Finally, a detailed agreement was drafted to protect national and company data. A memorandum of understanding (MoU) covering the U.K.-U.S. advanced STOVL (ASTOVL) project was signed on a wet day at Ames in January 1986.

The Yak-141's bifurcated rear end and three-bearing swivel nozzle foreshadowed the JSF design. But without the thrust-boosting lift fan it needed augmented thrust to hover— which precluded vertical landings on anything except a steel deck with a cooling system. At the Farnborough air show in 1992, it hovered but did not land vertically. Bill Sweetman

The U.S. Navy, in 1990, had no plans for anything resembling JSF. The service's most important warplane project was the McDonnell Douglas/General Dynamics A-12, essentially a carrier-based flying-wing stealth bomber with a 1,000-mile-class range and a massive internal weapon load. Lockheed Martin

The A-12 packed a 12,000 pound bomb load, plus two AGM-88 HARM missiles and two AMRAAMs. Weight problems, delays, and the Navy's failure to tell Defense Secretary Dick Cheney about the project's difficulties led to its cancellation, leaving a void in Navy plans. Lockheed Martin

Of the four chosen configurations, the most familiar was a P.1154-type design with a vectored thrust engine and PCB. It was well understood, but the noise, heat, and erosion the exhaust caused was a problem, and the location of the engine at the mid-point of the airframe militated against supersonic efficiency. The location of the jet nozzles against the fuselage sides was an inherent problem from the viewpoint of the emerging technology of stealth, which most people knew existed but few knew anything about.

Another simple approach was the remote augmented lift system (RALS), which had been under study since the 1970s. RALS used a conventional, rear-mounted engine with a vectoring nozzle; to balance the airplane in jet-borne flight, part of the air from the engine was ducted to a vertically-mounted afterburner in the nose. RALS allowed you to build a STOVL fighter that looked a lot like a CTOL fighter, but the hot, fast exhaust from the lift nozzle was intimidating.

Some NASA-Ames researchers still favored the ejector principle, despite its failure on the XFV-12. The de Havilland Canada company had designed a very different version of the concept with large ejectors built into the roots of a delta wing, and General Dynamics had designed a STOVL fighter, the E-7, which used some F-16 components.

The fourth concept, drawing attention from Rolls-Royce and Lockheed, was the tandem fan engine. This engine had two sets of fan stages, rotating on the same shaft, but separated by a long duct which incorporated valves and auxiliary inlets. In forward flight, the airflow passed through the fan and the core in series. In the hover, auxiliary exhausts and inlets opened and the fan and core operate with separate gas streams.

The plan was to select the most promising of the four proposals for further investigation, late in 1988. The United States and United Kingdom would then concentrate their resources on large-scale demonstrations of the chosen concept, with a view to being ready to start development of an operational aircraft in 1995. Industry teams drew up preliminary designs around each system, explored their technical challenges, and measured them against the users' needs.

The marines, potentially, had more money than other customers and therefore wielded the greatest influence on the requirement. By 1987, they decided that the ASTOVL would replace both the AV-8B and the F/A-18, so the

The USAF's priority project in the early 1990s was the Lockheed Martin F/A-22 Raptor supersonic stealth fighter—and that is still the case. But delays, cost increases, and tight budgets mean that the service is able to buy barely one-third as many airplanes as it wanted, forcing it to look for a smaller airplane to replace thousands of F-16s. Bill Sweetman

Better agility was one reason that the F/A-22 beat the Northrop YF-23 in the Advanced Tactical Fighter competition. But the YF-23 was faster and probably more stealthy, and its weapons bay, located in the fuselage aft of the cockpit, was deeper and more adaptable to other ordnance than the wide, flat bays of the F/A-22. Northrop Grumman

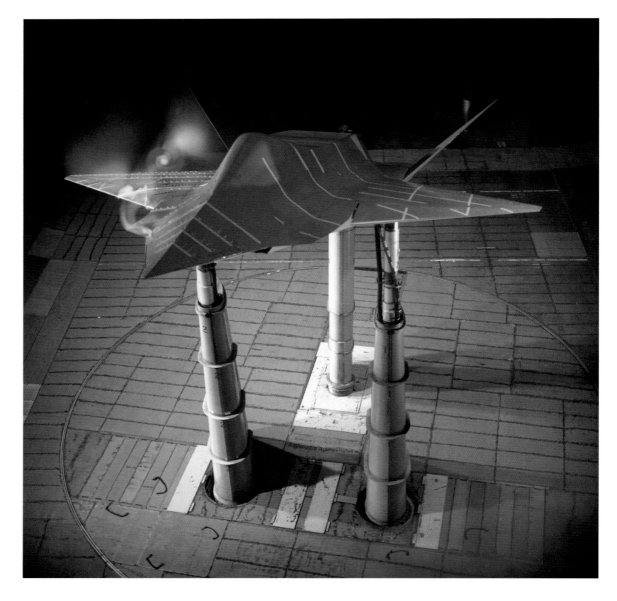

Sharc (subsonic, high-alpha research configuration) was a USAF Laboratory project for a stealthy, agile fighter using unconventional controls such as air jets that modulated lift over the wing. This 55 percent scale model was tested at NASA's Ames Research Center. NASA

marines would become an all-STOVL force, independent of the super-carriers. This meant that the marines would be in the market for at least 600 STOVL fighters, but it implied a tougher specification, including air-to-air and all-weather attack capability. The USMC decided to rebuild their AV-8Bs into an AV-8B Plus configuration, including a radar. That would extend the fighters' life into the early 2000s, when an ASTOVL aircraft could be ready.

Key features of the requirement included a maximum empty operating weight of 24,000 pounds—the same as an F/A-18—supersonic speed, stealth characteristics including the ability to carry some weapons internally, and an operating radius of 500 miles with about 6,000 pounds of offensive weapons.

Building on the Harrier coalition, the ASTOVL effort had put together many recognizable parts of today's joint strike

fighter program by 1987: the Anglo-American partnership, the Royal Navy and USMC commitment to the project, and the cardinal points of the requirement. But this was not as good as it looked, because there were real reasons why the project could not leave the ground.

First, none of the participants had enough money. The RN had a small requirement and the marines had no significant research and development money; it all belonged to the navy.

Secondly, transatlantic collaboration was hobbled by the secrecy surrounding stealth. Some of the ASTOVL concepts were less compatible with stealth than others, but those who knew this could not say so.

The U.S. Air Force and Navy had four stealthy combat aircraft in the works: the F-117 fighter was in service, the B-2 bomber was under construction, the A-12 carrier-based bomber was being designed, and Lockheed and Northrop were starting work on the advanced tactical fighter prototypes.

How Sharc got its name. Inlet design is always a challenge for a stealthy, agile fighter, and the radical serrated slot of the Sharc inlet was designed to combine stealth with good performance at high angles of attack. NASA

An MRF study configuration—resembling one of those looked at by McDonnell Douglas—under test in a NASA tunnel. In the early 1990s, some USAF leaders were strongly in favor of a super-stealthy, high-technology MRF. NASA

Even people working on one project had little knowledge of the others. The United Kingdom had a surprising level of awareness of stealth, at a government-to-government level. A RAF pilot was already flying F-117s out of Tonopah, Nevada, even though U.S. citizens weren't supposed to know that the airplane existed but that firewalls protected knowledge in the United Kingdom and most engineers at BAe did not even know about the United Kingdom's access.

The principal problem, though, was that each of the ASTOVL candidate concepts had at least one ineradicable limitation that was intolerable to the customer. PCB was unworkable in terms of ground erosion and hot gas recirculation, and was incompatible with stealth. RALS was a good way to dig a post-hole. Nobody knew how to get the ejector concept to transition successfully, or how to build the complex valves in the heart of the tandem fan engine. And, apart from the marines and the RN, nobody appeared to give a hoot. By 1989, the ASTOVL effort seemed to be grinding to a halt, lost in a developmental Valley of Death.

If the Pentagon has a patron saint of lost causes, it is the Defense Advanced Research Projects Agency (DARPA). Formed after the Soviet Union shocked the United States with the launch of Sputnik 1, DARPA's mission is to explore and foster technologies that the individual services may have neglected. One of DARPA's greatest successes was its early and crucial support of stealth technology.

In the 1960s, the agency invented a way to use computers to share information about research and development efforts. It was called Arpanet, and this was the direct precursor of the Internet.

DARPA had been peripherally involved in the ASTOVL program since 1986. The director of DARPA's advanced systems technology office, Ron Murphy, had a long background in V/STOL. In fact, when he joined DARPA to run a classified program in 1984, many people assumed incorrectly that it

NASA LANGLEY
16 FOOT TRANSONIC TUNNEL

Boeing proposed this broad-winged, four-tail design for the Navy's AX program, intended successor to the A-12, but a single-service, single-mission design stood little chance with post-Cold War budgets. NASA

The earlier study had set performance targets. DARPA's requirement made only two firm demands, both related to cost and operability: the aircraft should have an empty weight not higher than 24,000 pounds (10,900 kg)—a rough and ready way of capping the cost—and should take up no more room on a carrier deck than an F/A-18. Otherwise, DARPA looked for the best possible balance of range, speed, and stealth.

Another key feature of the DARPA requirement was that it was based on the General Electric F120 and Pratt & Whitney YF119 engines and was then tested on the Lockheed YF-22 and Northrop YF-23 advanced tactical fighter (ATF) prototypes. These powerful engines opened up new approaches for ASTOVL designs. In particular, they made it possible for an F-18-sized fighter with a single engine to land vertically without using afterburning or RALS.

From 1990 onward, the Pentagon was increasing DARPA's budgets and encouraging the agency to focus on making weapons more affordable. To help manage and promote the emerging ASTOVL project, DARPA hired a consultant, Dr. Bill Scheuren. He was a retired marine colonel

This large twin-engine, two-seat airplane was proposed by Lockheed to meet the joint-service A/F-X requirement, which succeeded AX in 1992. A/F-X was intended to replace the F-14, the subsonic A-6, the F-111, and, eventually, the F-117 and F-15E. Lockheed Martin

RIGHT: Derived from the F-22, and using a great deal of similar technology in terms of avionics and propulsion, the Lockheed A/F-X design had a swing wing and deeper weapons bays capable of accommodating 2,000-pound bombs. Lockheed Martin

was a V/STOL effort. In 1988, according to DARPA program manager Chuck Heber, the agency realized that the U.S./U.K. program was in trouble and started working to generate a requirement "since there was no way otherwise to go ahead." DARPA persuaded the navy and marines to authorize a "desired operational capability document," an extremely tentative requirement. Heber would remark later, "That and 50 cents buys you a cup of coffee."

DARPA's emphasis was different from the U.S./U.K. study. Most importantly, DARPA wanted to build and fly a prototype as soon as possible, after a fast-paced ground technology demonstration. DARPA managers believed that such a fast-paced approach had been the secret to its early success with stealth. The demonstrator served two roles: it persuaded industry that there might be money in the new concept, and it forced the designers to offer solutions that were practical.

The swing wing provided the A/F-X design with a modest approach speed even at high landing weights, and the great wingspan provided plenty of room for control surfaces. But the airplane would have been large and expensive to buy and operate. Both MRF and A/F-X were terminated in early 1993. Lockheed Martin

who had been one of the first five USMC officers to evaluate the Harrier; Scheuren would become a key player as DARPA sought support for a demonstrator program.

Between 1989 and 1991, DARPA funded aircraft design studies by McDonnell Douglas, General Dynamics, and Lockheed Advanced Development Company (the Skunk Works), together with propulsion studies at General Electric and P&W.

The studies concentrated on two of the problems that had doomed the earlier STOVL concepts: the hot, high-velocity exhaust gas with the associated dangers of ground erosion, flying debris, and hot gas ingestion. Stealth appeared to mandate a single, rear-mounted exhaust nozzle in up-and-away flight.

DARPA also recognized that the war-fighter's requirements were changing. After the first Gulf War, it was clear that future conflicts would involve a much higher proportion of smart weapons. They would be too expensive to be dumped if the mission was aborted, so the aircraft would have to be able to land vertically with a significant weapon load. This required a greater margin of vertical thrust over empty weight than the Harrier enjoyed.

All these problems could be solved if there was a way to move some of the engine's total energy forward and to balance the rear-mounted nozzle, while increasing the system's mass flow and thrust, reducing its jet velocity.

Lockheed Skunk Works engineer Paul Bevilaqua devised such a method, which was patented in 1993. He had

Meeting service requirements in the early 1990s was difficult because the services themselves had little idea what they wanted or what they could afford. Lockheed Martin's Skunk Works weighed into the battle with a radically modified F-117 with new outer wings and bigger weapon bays. Lockheed Martin

The re-winged F-117 would have featured off-the-shelf F414 engines, lighter stealth materials, and a more normal canopy than the basic F-117 and would have carried a radar. Prototypes would have been modified from F-117As, saving time and money. *Lockheed Martin*

Radically changing an airplane by giving it a new wing was nothing new to Lockheed. Flown in 1983, the F-16XL combined a stretched fuselage with an arrow wing derived from supersonic transport research. Doubled fuel capacity combined with more efficient stores carriage—bombs were carried in tandem, not in draggy clusters—vastly increased its range. NASA

evolved the system from the tandem fan, with three principal differences: the forward fan stream was separate from the core airflow at all times; the fan was shut down in cruising flight; and the fan was installed so that its axis was vertical. It was a less complex system than the tandem fan and had a more easily controlled transition. With its driveshaft and gears, it was also reminiscent of Michel Wibault's Gyropter.

General Electric dusted off the data on lift fan systems that it had built for the U.S. Army's XV-5A in the 1960s. Turbines drove the GE fans, fed by engine exhaust gas. They were designed with a higher thrust, smaller diameter than the wide, and shallow fans on the XV-5.

Both the gas-coupled lift fan (GCLF) and shaft-driven lift-fan (SDLF) attracted the attention of Scheuren's researchers at DARPA. They promised a cool environment, a conventional-looking airplane in forward flight and boosted thrust, without a high jet velocity for vertical landing.

In a parallel study early in 1990, the USAF's Flight Dynamics laboratory issued STOVL study contracts to General Dynamics, McDonnell Douglas, Lockheed, and Northrop under the advanced fighter technology integration (AFTI) program but cancelled them a few months later when it became clear that Air Combat Command had no interest in STOVL. But in the process some of the contractors reopened the files on lift-plus-lift/cruise (LPLC) designs, with a vertically mounted jet engine behind the cockpit.

Behind all these low-profile studies was an uncertain picture for future fighter planning. In 1990, there were two big new fighter programs under way. Northrop and Lockheed were getting ready to fly prototypes of the advanced tactical fighter (ATF); Lockheed's F-22 would be selected as the winner in 1991. The navy was developing the McDonnell Douglas/General Dynamics A-12 carrier-based attack aircraft. The smaller F-16 was still in production for the USAF and the F/A-18 for the navy.

Development of improved versions of the navy's F-14 and A-6 had been curtailed.

Some senior people within the Office of the Secretary of Defense (OSD), though, were concerned that service plans were short-changing the fighter export market, which the United States had dominated for 15 years with the F-16 and F/A-18. These airplanes had no direct successors. The Soviet Union—both the traditional threat and the supplier to second-level threats—had developed two new and formidable fighters, the MiG-29 and Su-27, and was showing even willingness to export them since the fall of the Iron Curtain.

Traditional competitors in Europe were developing new fighters, the Saab Gripen, Dassault Rafale, and EuroFighter EFA, that were due to be on the market in the mid-1990s. The new ATF and A-12 were large, expensive, specialized, included sensitive stealth technology, and would not be candidates for export to most countries. The concern was that the European airplanes would replace the F-16 and F/A-18.

In early 1991, Defense Secretary Dick Cheney abruptly canceled the A-12. The navy urgently needed a new fighter with greater war-load than the existing F/A-18, to replace the aging F-14 and A-6. The chosen solution, pleasing to

the navy F/A-18 community and the OSD, was the scaled-up F/A-18E/F Super Hornet, placed under contract in 1992. The navy, though, did not believe that the Super Hornet was the definitive substitute for the A-12; it was too small and not stealthy and issued a requirement for a long-range, heavy-payload attack aircraft, named A-X. With diminished post-Cold War budgets there was no way the navy could afford the project alone, and it accordingly became a joint USAF/navy project known as A/F-X.

By 1992, three fighter projects were in the works: the F-22, the Super Hornet, and A/F-X, but none of them would replace the F-16, either in the USAF or in export markets. The 1993 defense budget included money for industry to work on an F-16 replacement, known as the multi-role fighter (MRF).

There were two ways to do MRF: with a radically improved F-16 or an all-new aircraft. In early 1993, Air Combat Command Leader General Mike Loh spoke strongly in favor of a development approach, which he called "rollover-plus." This involved replacing an in-service airplane, not with a brand-new design, but with a thoroughly modernized version of the existing aircraft. General Dynamics responded with a delta-winged F-16 with a stretched fuselage and almost doubled internal fuel capacity.

Lockheed's shaft-driven lift-fan concept was tested in 1996 at near-full-scale on this large scale powered model (LSPM). Fitted with an F100 engine, the LSPM could not demonstrate transition, but it featured a shaft-driven fan, a deflected cruise nozzle and auxiliary inlets. Lockheed Martin

LEFT: The F-16XL concept was revived in 1995 for the F-16U, offered to the United Arab Emirates, although the wing was based on that of the F-22. The UAE insisted that the USAF should commit to the delta-winged fighter, though, and the USAF would not do so. Aside from stealth, the F-16U would have equaled the JSF in some respects and surpassed it in others. Bill Sweetman

The goal of the LSPM was to avoid the unpredictable, too-complex-to-model snakes in the grass that had killed many STOVL programs. In particular, the researchers wanted to look at hot gas recirculation and jet effects on the ground. Here, the model is being prepared for low-forward-speed tests in NASA's 80x120-foot tunnel. Lockheed Martin

Full-power tests of the LSPM were carried out at NASA's Outdoor Aerodynamic Research Facility at Ames. Here, the model could be lowered to the point where its wheels would touch the ground, with the engine and fan running. Lockheed Martin

Loh's boss, air force Chief of Staff General Merrill McPeak, favored an all-new MRF. It would take longer and cost more, but it would offer all-round stealth, which with no amount of modification could be added to an F-16. Spurred by the air force requirement, aerospace companies started to position themselves to win an MRF competition.

Keenest were the companies that had lost to Lockheed and its teammates, General Dynamics and Boeing, in the ATF competition. Northrop launched internal studies of single-engine fighters that resembled its ATF contender, the YF-23. McDonnell Douglas turned its advanced-design group into an entire new division, the Phantom Works, with the aim of winning MRF and other new stealth-related programs. The company's work emphasized ultra-stealthy tailless designs, along with techniques for building prototypes and small-run production aircraft quickly and cheaply.

None of the new fighters were what the marines needed and this gave Scheuren and the DARPA planners an opportunity. What they needed was a service customer and end user to say that they would use an ASTOVL, if it were built. Naval Air Systems Command (Navair) might still view STOVL with distrust, but it could not ignore the need to replace aging marine aircraft. DARPA persuaded the navy to draft a preliminary requirement for a marine ASTOVL, also known as the STOVL strike fighter (SSF), and this allowed DARPA to start spending money on it.

Later, one of the DARPA managers expressed the view that the only reason that Navair went along with the plan was that Navair expected the first round of studies to show that the STOVL fighter would not work. "We rolled them," he remarked. "Navair didn't expect a positive result."

DARPA laid out a plan for STOVL development. After about a year of competitive design studies, DARPA choose two teams to carry out a ground test program, running from March 1993 to March 1996, building and testing near-full-size, powered models of two different ASTOVL designs. The main goal was to avoid building a dud like the Rockwell

Dye streaks under the LSPM show that one predicted effect of the lift-fan system has been achieved: the relatively cool exhaust from the lift fan has blocked the hot gas from the aft nozzle and has kept it behind the inlets. Lockheed Martin

XFV-12A. The models would be tested on a massive gantry rig at Ames, where they could run their engines and lift fans tens of feet off the ground, measuring the lift produced by their engines and checking the engineers' predictions of complex phenomena such as hot-gas-ingestion.

In mid-1996, DARPA would pick the most promising concept and award a contract to build and fly two proto-types by the end of 1999. At that point, the customer would be able to launch development of an operational aircraft at an acceptable level of risk.

Before the contracts were awarded, a new element was added to the ASTOVL program. The DARPA team recognized that the fan-boosted ASTOVL concepts could be modified into a conventional fighter by removing the lift hardware and substituting a fuel tank. The result would be a fighter with a better range than the F-16, which was precisely what the USAF wanted in an MRF.

Before the JAST effort started, McDonnell Douglas had formed the Phantom Works in an effort to position itself for a future low-observable fighter. One result was the X-36, a secret prototype declassified in 1996. Eliminating the vertical tails substantially reduced it's all-round RCS. NASA

The X-36, a small unmanned prototype with a cruise-missile engine, flew successfully. Directional control was provided by differential drag devices on the wing trailing edges and a thrust-vectoring nozzle. McDonnell Douglas

RIGHT: The X-36 in flight later in its test program (it now says Boeing on the side) with its trailing-edge surfaces snapped open as airbrakes. The yaw-only vectoring nozzle was a unique low-observable design with no external moving parts. NASA

A small jet-effects model of McDonnell Douglas' ASTOVL concept, with its gas-coupled lift fan. The design also featured a separate nozzle for the lift-cruise engine with retractable switch-in vectoring nozzles in the rear fuselage. NASA

The prospect of replacing the marine's F/A-18s and AV-8s and USAF F-16s with a common aircraft was important, because it linked ASTOVL to DARPA's strategic goal of making weapons less costly. A dual-service fighter could save tens of billions of dollars in research, development, and production. The project acquired a new name: common affordable lightweight fighter (CALF).

DARPA awarded the first CALF contracts to McDonnell Douglas and Lockheed in March 1993. Both companies proposed stealthy canard designs with internal bays for two 2,000-pound (900 kg) bombs and a pair of AIM-120 air-to-air missiles, and with auxiliary lift fans located behind the cockpit.

Lockheed's design used a modified P&W F119 engine. A clutch immediately in front of the engine connected the low-pressure shaft to a driveshaft, which drove an Allison-developed fan. McDonnell Douglas planned to use a version of the GE F120, modified to allow high-pressure air to be bled from the compressor. The air would be ducted forward to the lift-fan's turbine. In both concepts, the total airflow was almost doubled in the vertical lift mode, boosting low-speed thrust and reducing jet velocity.

Both teams designed prototype aircrafts that could be built in two versions: one with its lift system and one without. The designation X-32 was assigned; the conventional take-off and landing (CTOL) aircraft would be the X-32A, and the STOVL aircraft would be the X-32B, whichever team was selected.

From the outset, DARPA planned to involve the United Kingdom in the program. After some delays due to the sensitivity of stealth technology, the United Kingdom formally joined the effort in early 1994. British Aerospace, long associated with McDonnell Douglas on the Harrier, teamed with the U.S. company to support ASTOVL.

CALF was an outside bet because there was still no formal requirement for an ASTOVL aircraft or a CTOL derivative in early 1993, but the potential jackpot was large enough to bring two more contenders into the fray.

For Boeing, CALF was a golden opportunity. Boeing had never built a manned supersonic airplane or a jet fighter. It had not delivered a fighter to the air force since the 1930s; it had not in fact, delivered any manned combat airplane in 30 years. But as a defense contractor, it had a tremendous reputation for tackling difficult assignments like the E-3 AWACS airborne-early-warning airplane, and it had narrowly missed out on winning a number of major competitions.

In the early 1980s, the company used money from surging jetliner sales to boost its military division. Boeing invested in new facilities, including an outdoor radar cross-section testing range at Boardman in northern Oregon, and a sophisticated, ultra-secure indoor range at Boeing Field. Its fighter team placed fourth in the ATF demonstration/validation contest in 1986, beating McDonnell Douglas and earning a place on the winning Lockheed team.

Boeing started looking at future fighters as soon as the ATF award went to Lockheed in April 1991. Convinced that future post-Cold War budgets would be tight, Boeing focused on low cost. The company concluded that what was needed was a multi-service, multi-purpose, long-range fighter with an empty weight close to that of an F-16 and STOVL capability to replace the Harrier.

In 1993, Boeing released a few details of its new fighter: a compact and radical delta-wing design, smaller than the Lockheed and McDonnell Douglas designs. Although it did not win the DARPA contract, the company had enough faith in its concept to build and test a large, powered model with its own funds.

In 1993, Northrop was in the process of rebuilding itself. The company had expanded massively to build the B-2 but ended up with contracts for only 21 airplanes and a pile of money. This money was used to buy Grumman, and Northrop announced its intention to bid on CALF in the summer of

1994. Northrop Grumman chose an LPLC design that featured an unusual "hammerhead" wing planform with a small canard attached to a large fixed leading-edge extension. Northrop did not intend to build a powered model, arguing that the risks of the lift-plus-lift/cruise configuration were small. (In fact, a lift-plus-lift/cruise supersonic STOVL fighter had already flown: Russia's Yakovlev Yak-141, the existence of which was revealed in 1991.)

Seismic shifts in Pentagon policy were about to change the CALF program beyond all recognition.

The presidential election of 1992 ended 12 years of Republican rule and brought new leadership to the Pentagon. One figure stood head and shoulders above a mostly mediocre group of appointees: Dr. Bill Perry, who returned to the Pentagon as deputy secretary of defense and became defense secretary in early 1994, after Les Aspin resigned. Known as "the godfather of stealth," because of his role in launching the original stealth programs in the late 1970s, Perry was an entrepreneur and engineer who realized that Cold War business-as-usual was dead.

McDonnell Douglas' early ASTOVL design: this concept, released in 1994, may have been censored by adding tails because the X-36 was still secret at the time. Note the separate, two-dimensional cruise nozzle, an indicator of the degree of stealth planned for the design.
McDonnell Douglas

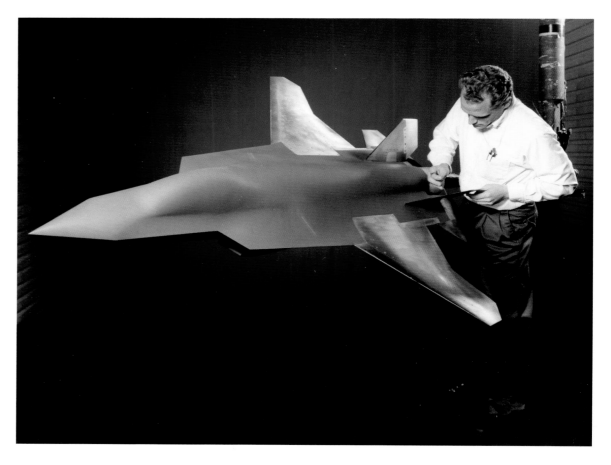

By 1995, with a carrier-landing requirement added to the original ASTOVL specification, McDonnell Douglas had switched to a "lambda" wing, rather than a delta, and small aft tails. Under the skin, a bigger change: the bulky and vulnerable gas-driven fan had been replaced by a separate lift-jet engine in the same location.
McDonnell Douglas

From now on, Perry believed, the United States would not buy unique weapons for each service unless it was absolutely necessary. Moreover, the Pentagon could not sustain half-a-dozen prime contractors for every type of weapon, which was still the case for fighters in 1993. The Pentagon paid the bills for this redundancy through "independent research and development" funds built into the overhead for other contracts. Perry's message was brutal: consolidate or die.

In a September 1993 Pentagon review of defense programs, the MRF and the A/F-X were cancelled. Instead, the Pentagon would establish a new program, called joint advanced strike technology (JAST). The JAST office was to define and develop aircraft, weapon, and sensor technologies that would support the development of future tactical aircraft.

In December 1993, when the Anglo-American ASTOVL community held its biennial conference in Santa Clara,

California, nobody quite knew what to make of JAST; the JAST office itself had not formally opened its doors, and speakers avoided linking JAST with DARPA's CALF program. CALF was clearly a prime example of what JAST was supposed to do, but the ASTOVL advocates—with a funded flight demonstration program within their grasp—feared that Congress or the Pentagon would gut CALF and assign its goals to the JAST office, where ASTOVL might languish for years.

Alternatively, JAST and CALF could be seen as complementary; while JAST would focus on operational issues, weapons, and sensors, CALF was strictly an aircraft and propulsion demonstration. Other people in the industry were openly critical of JAST, worried that it would turn into an "engineering sandbox" which would fritter resources on new ideas that would not reflect the users' operational needs.

Those who doubted that JAST would amount to anything reckoned without the program's first director, USAF Major General George Muellner. A 5,300 hour fighter pilot with 690 combat missions over Vietnam in F-4s, Muellner had once commanded the 6513th Test Squadron, based at the USAF's secret flight-test center in Groom Lake, Nevada. In the Gulf War, Muellner assembled and led the scratch unit of USAF and civilian technicians which took the experimental Joint STARS radar surveillance system into action.

By the fall of 1994, CALF was indeed about to be absorbed by JAST but, under Muellner's leadership, it had become JAST's centerpiece. Muellner's vision was to create a family of aircrafts to cover all the operational needs that were to have been met by CALF, A/F-X, and MRF. Using new technology to reduce costs in development, manufacture, and operation, the JAST family would have the performance and survivability to perform deep-strike missions but would be affordable enough to replace F-16s in the United States and overseas. Such a "universal fighter" could be built in the thousands, reducing costs.

Perhaps the most important element of the new approach was Gulf War experience. Although some observers believed that the impact of smart weapons on the conflict had been exaggerated, and it was true that only a minority of the bombs dropped during the conflict were laser-guided, one fact could not be denied: a disproportionate amount of damage to Iraqi capabilities was caused by fighters carrying three bombs: stealthy F-117s, older F-111s, and F-15Es. The A-12 design had been driven by the need to carry 12,000 pounds of bombs internally, The A/F-X was intended to carry some 8,000 pounds in its weapon bays, but there were reasons for arguing that a 4,000-pound internal load would be ample for most missions. This had a vast impact on the size of the airplane.

The JAST office adopted state-of-the-art industrial processes and tools to pursue its ambitious goals. The elements of the program were organized into integrated product teams (IPTs) which combined engineers, production, and maintenance experts from the contractors and the customers. The goal was to avoid designing technically inspiring devices that were too expensive to produce or impossible to maintain. JAST would be designed on computers using commercially available design tools, and the

JAST team enthusiastically adopted the Internet and the Web as tools of communication.

It was clear that the information revolution was going to have a profound effect on the cost and performance of the fighter's onboard electronics. What was definitely not clear was exactly what that impact would be. In 1995, the Internet was in widespread use but it had yet to make its mark on commerce or to emerge as a medium in its own right alongside print or TV. There was a wide gulf between the products of the consumer electronics industry and the requirements of military users. Commercial off-the-shelf (COTS) technology was more of a dream than reality. However, one important principle was that technology would make it possible for complex missions to be performed by a single-seat fighter.

Another important tool was later distributed: interactive simulation. The JAST office conducted war-games that involved experts and resources from all services and throughout the United States, using simulators connected by satellite. This made it possible to evaluate the actual benefits of the airplane's performance to the joint-force

The final McDonnell Douglas JAST design—developed with the support of British Aerospace and Northrop Grumman—featured a "near-tailless" layout. The shallow-angled tail surfaces made only a small contribution to directional stability and none to control. The pitch/yaw vectoring nozzle added to the fighter's agility, but the design could fly safely without it. McDonnell Douglas

A separate lift engine occupied a bay behind the cockpit of McDonnell Douglas' STOVL JAST design. Note one advantage of the separate vectoring nozzles of the lift-cruise engine: the afterbody shape is extremely clean, optimized for up-and-away flight. McDonnell Douglas

One of Muellner's tasks was to investigate the navy's insistence on a twin-engine aircraft. The JAST office sponsored an exhaustive analysis of the one-versus-two-engine issue, performed by Georgia Tech Research Institute and Johns Hopkins University—academic engineering centers with, respectively, long-standing air force and navy links. The conclusion was that the single-engine aircraft would be equal or better in terms of survivability. The only time that a twin can survive a hit that would down a single-engine type is if one engine is knocked out, but the other engine and all other vital systems are left intact. The studies showed that this would hardly ever happen. (It did not work that way for Muellner, who ejected from a battle-damaged F-4 over Vietnam.)

It took more than studies and simulation, though, to persuade the services to buy commonality. Hard reality did the job. The navy needed a stealth aircraft. The marines' AV-8Bs were not getting younger. The USAF would not maintain even its post-1993 force size without a low-cost F-16 replacement. Individual leaders might have their reservations about Muellner's vision, but they had no alternatives either.

By the spring of 1995, the JAST train was moving at express speed. In an interview in April, Muellner said that the customers had converged on a family of closely similar designs, different mainly in the way that they landed and took-off.

CALF had been important in this process; it was the nucleus around which the JAST requirement formed. The work already done by DARPA and its contractors pointed to a common solution for the marines and the USAF. The single-versus-twin study removed the main obstacle in the way of adapting the design for the navy.

But JAST would differ from CALF in important respects. JAST was oriented toward the requirements of three U.S. customers, while CALF had been inspired by the USMC, so performance and other specifications would change to meet the other services needs.

JAST would also be tied more closely to operational goals than CALF had been. JAST was aimed at reducing risks for a military aircraft, and included many elements beyond the ASTOVL systems. The flight demonstrators would not carry these technologies, but would represent a design that would accommodate them.

campaign. Was it worth increasing the range at the expense of maximum Mach number? What was the actual value of longer-range radar? The war-gaming tools provided a consistent answer, and were critical as the customer services; the marines, the USAF, the U.S. Navy, and, soon, the Royal Navy, began to hammer out a joint requirement.

If there was one element of JAST that aroused skepticism and hostility, it was the idea that one aircraft could work for every service. The last time this had been tried at the Pentagon's direction, the result had been the F-111. Top-level officials, chiefly Secretary of Defense Robert McNamara, had become fixated on maintaining commonality between the airframes of the navy and air force versions of the fighter. The navy had rejected the aircraft, leaving the USAF with an aircraft burdened with design compromises.

In the case of JAST, it seemed impossible that the navy's deep-strike fighter and the USAF's F-16 replacement could be remotely similar. But any aircraft powered by a modified F119 or F120 was not exactly small, and the long range required by the USAF was close to the navy's needs.

Because JAST was directly linked to an engineering, manufacturing, and development (EMD) program, the program office wanted to keep it competitive, so the office decided to fly prototypes of two designs. (DARPA had planned to fly only one.) The two candidates would be selected in the second half of 1996.

The industrial implications were enormous. The marines wanted to replace 600 older aircraft, the navy needed 300 aircraft, and the USAF could replace almost 2,000 F-16s. Never had such a massive program been created so fast. Moreover, JAST looked like the only U.S. tactical aircraft program that would start before 2010.

In 1986, seven companies competed to build the USAF's ATF prototypes. By the end of 1994, under the pressure of the Pentagon's drive towards consolidation, two of those had disappeared by merger. Grumman, its major combat aircraft programs all terminated, was acquired by Northrop. General Dynamics disassembled itself, selling the F-16 line in Fort Worth to Lockheed, which was in the process of merging with Martin-Marietta. Rockwell had virtually left the military aircraft business. This left four U.S. companies in the race: Lockheed Martin, Boeing, McDonnell Douglas, and Northrop Grumman.

In the ATF competition, most of the competitors had teamed-up, so five out of seven competitors eventually shared the demonstration/validation contracts. Late in 1994, Northrop Grumman agreed to collaborate with McDonnell Douglas and BAe on JAST. The three companies formed a "dream team." It encompassed all the Western world's operational STOVL experience; both the surviving groups with carrier-based fighter skills, McDonnell Douglas and Grumman; Northrop's stealth technology; and Grumman's and McDonnell Douglas' expertise in all-weather strike systems. British Aerospace was engaged in a secret project called Replica, which was intended to culminate in the construction of a detailed RCS model of a stealthy fighter.

Boeing and Lockheed talked about teaming. This would have left only two teams to bid for the two prototype contracts, eliminating competition. However, the JAST program office indicated that it did not want to review multiple designs from each team; the teams would have to make their pitches based on a single design.

Neither Boeing nor Lockheed would give up its own design. They proceeded as competitors into JAST, a decision that would have a massive impact on the U.S. aerospace industry. Lockheed was clearly in a strong position, with one of the DARPA contracts in hand and its experience on the F-22 and F-16. Boeing was an outsider. But the creators of the company's JAST design were confident that they had a better mousetrap. The creators believed that they could win one of the demonstration contracts on their own, and that they would win the final selection; their bosses believed them.

Many people—including some McDonnell Douglas people at St. Louis—considered the outcome of a three-way contest to be a foregone conclusion. It wasn't just a question of Boeing's lack of experience with supersonic airplanes or fighters. Established fighter manufacturers like Lockheed Martin or McDonnell Douglas had long-standing connections with their customers. Their executive ranks, particularly on the marketing side, were salted with former fighter pilots, and many of them were retired generals or admirals. The best of them were commanders who had earned the respect of contemporaries and juniors alike, and were an invaluable source of intelligence about what the user community really wanted. Boeing, it was felt, could produce an admirable solution to the JAST requirement from an engineering viewpoint, but they'd have trouble selling it to pilots.

If there's one thing in this business, which will kill you every time, aside from ground impact, it's complacency. McDonnell Douglas' actions in the run-up to the selection of two JAST competitors bespoke its confidence that the contest was a formality.

In June 1995, only a year before the planned down-select date, the McDonnell Douglas team abandoned the gas-driven lift fan in favor of LPLC. The nearly complete, large-scale, powered model of the GCLF design was mothballed. Late in the game, the designers had realized that the gas-coupled system was uniquely vulnerable to combat damage. Located on the top part of section of the fuselage used for fuel tanks, the ducts carried hot, high-pressure gas. Even a small puncture caused by a projectile or warhead fragment—most anti-aircraft warheads are of the blast-fragmentation type, like a grenade—could cause a fire when the pilot attempted to start the fan. Even with a means to detect a punctured duct before landing, the damaged airplane could not land on a ship.

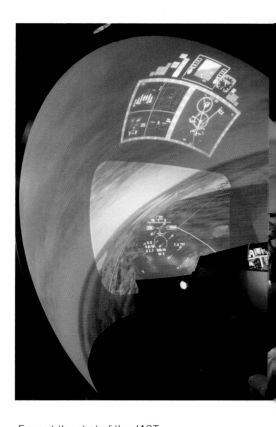

Even at the start of the JAST program, advanced simulation technology was used both to evaluate cockpit displays and— by linking with other simulators— provide an opportunity to see how different JAST capabilities would affect an air campaign.
McDonnell Douglas

Boeing indicated in 1993 that it was getting into the ASTOVL battle, although some of the features of the AVX-70 design are suppressed in this artist's concept—absent are the wing-tip fins, abbreviated nose, and hippo-jaw inlet. Boeing

The driveshaft on Lockheed Martin's aircraft also represented a single point of vulnerability, but it was much smaller than the gas ducts and was housed in the center of the airplane where the rest of the structure protected it from damage.

In many respects, LPLC was not a bad solution. It had the smallest vulnerable area of any design. It eliminated the volume and weight of the power transmission system, whether gas or mechanical. The lift jet would be at least competitive in terms of weight with the remotely-driven lift fan: even in the late 1960s, Rolls-Royce and Allison had demonstrated the XJ99, a lift engine delivering 9,000 pounds of thrust and weighing under 500 pounds.

An LPLC aircraft would work with a stock F119 engine fitted with a simple vectoring nozzle, removing an entire engine development effort. The lift engine and main

engine could be developed separately, which might make it easier to improve the airplane later.

By 1995, for example, General Electric and Allison were working on an advanced fighter engine with a variable bypass ratio, a small augmentor, and a physically fixed "flu-idic" vectoring nozzle, in which the gas stream could be directed by injecting fan air at its periphery. By drastically reducing the use of the augmentor, it would boost a fighter's range by as much as 40 percent. The new engine would not be ready for the first JAST deliveries, but it would be easier to incorporate in an LPLC than in a shaft-driven system.

But LPLC had drawbacks. The USMC's logistics community hated the idea of a fighter with two different engines. "The logistics people start climbing the walls, and rightly," Scheuren had said in 1991. "The care and feeding of one engine is bad enough." Another disadvantage was reliability.

On one mission, an LPLC fighter has three engine cycles: the lift/cruise engine starts and stops once and the lift engine twice, but unlike a conventional twin-engine fighter, it cannot land on the ship if either engine fails.

The McDonnell Douglas team still took some time to produce its definitive design. The company was working on a number of classified programs, including tailless demonstrators that had started in the early MRF days. Declassified in 1996, the X-36 was a small, pilotless demonstrator for an ultra-stealthy, agile supersonic fighter. It had a canard and a so-called "lambda" wing with a sharply kinked trailing edge and no vertical tail at all. Differential-drag surfaces on the trailing edge of the wing provided yaw control. With the aid of a fluidic vectoring nozzle, the X-36 configuration was the basis for the McDonnell Douglas team's third-to-last configuration in late 1995.

Both McDonnell Douglas and Lockheed Martin moved away from canard designs as the deadline approached. The main reason was the navy, which wanted the JSF to be able to land on the carrier with as large a weapon load as possible. This meant a bigger wing to keep approach speeds down at higher weights. This in turn meant more powerful control surfaces, to provide the pilot with fast and accurate control of the airplane's vertical flight-path. Both these create problems for a canard layout. The bigger wing extends further forward along the body and starts to compete for space with the large fore-planes. The big fore-planes create an ugly bump in the nose-to-tail distribution of the airplane's total cross-section, increasing transonic drag.

Anti-canard prejudice played a role. Lockheed had relocated the JAST program to the former General Dynamics plant at Fort Worth, where F-16 designer Harry Hillaker had long taught that "the optimum location for a canard is on somebody else's airplane." In 1995, the canard EuroFighter Typhoon was sitting on the ground while its designers wrestled with flight-control problems, and the Saab Gripen's developers were dealing with a rash of handling gremlins. All in all, the Lockheed Martin team felt that there was enough risk in the JAST program without adding a canard to the mix.

However, there was a distinct difference in the tail-aft designs that the companies produced. Lockheed Martin

looked at a pure delta wing; at one point, the company was looking at a delta for the USMC, USAF, RN, and a tailed configuration for the U.S. Navy—but the final design had four tails and a cropped delta wing. Data from the large-scale powered model was unveiled in April 1995, and it tested was at NASA Ames. It was still applicable.

Lockheed Martin's JSF design rapidly evolved to resemble the F-22. Like the F-22, its stealth design was a combination of flat, canted surfaces with large-radius curves on the wing, tails, and upper surfaces; like the F-22, it had four relatively large tail surfaces with the horizontal surfaces extending well past the jet exhausts. Lockheed Martin could back up both its stealth and performance projections by reference to the F-22, including flight tests of the YF-22 demonstrator.

McDonnell Douglas' final design was more radical. It had no separate vertical tails, and the horizontal surfaces were installed at such a shallow V-angle that they would be largely ineffective for yaw control; the same had been true of the V-tails on Northrop's YF-23 fighter prototype. The main engine nozzle would boost the fighter's maneuverability, vectoring the thrust in yaw and pitch, but flying qualities without thrust vectoring would be adequate for a carrier landing.

Boeing took the challenge of the navy requirement head-on, without changing its basic design. Instead, the company scaled the airplane up, fitted extended wingtips in place of tip-mounted fins, and added a range of high-lift devices to reduce approach speeds.

In March 1996, JAST office released a request for proposals (RFP) for the JAST prototypes, with a deadline in early June. Shortly afterward, the project's name formally changed from JAST to the joint strike fighter (JSF), reflecting the fact that it was backed by an operational requirement.

The JSF announcement was first set for late October, but then slipped to November 16, after the Presidential election. Briefing the media at the 1996 Farnborough air show, the McDonnell Douglas team seemed sure of success. Other observers, including the author, were less sure of the outcome.

Since 1970, the USAF had run several two-airplane demonstrator programs. In at least three cases, the lightweight fighter, advanced medium STOL transport projects

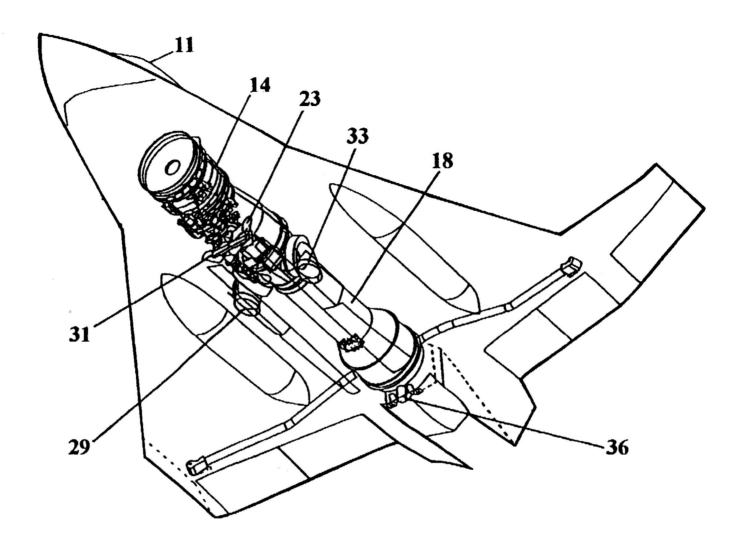

The biggest secret in Boeing's JAST concept—unveiled in this patent drawing—was that the engine was in the front, a feature not seen since some early Russian jet fighters. That allowed Boeing to balance the entire weight of the airplane on a simple pair of vectoring nozzles at the mid-body position. Boeing

in the 1970s, and the advanced tactical fighter in the 1980s, the service had set a pattern. The evaluators picked candidates that were different from one another and tended to select one low-risk candidate and one that offered greater payoffs but relied on innovative technology. For example, the Northrop YF-17 was a twin-engine aircraft with conventional flight controls, while the GD YF-16 was a single-engine, fly-by-wire design. Boeing's LWF actually placed second to the F-16, but it was not chosen because it was too much like the F-16, and the YF-17 would demonstrate a different approach to the requirement.

If the JSF evaluators followed this pattern, it was Boeing that was a sure bet. Boeing was offering a simpler airplane without a lift fan or engine, and with a very different wing, engine location, and inlet. Overall, too, the Boeing JSF was regarded as a high-risk design. If any of the features did not work properly, the airplane might fail to meet key areas of the requirement.

This left Lockheed Martin and McDonnell Douglas in contention for the other contract. If the evaluators stayed with the pattern, they would select the less risky design to compete with the radical Boeing approach. McDonnell

46

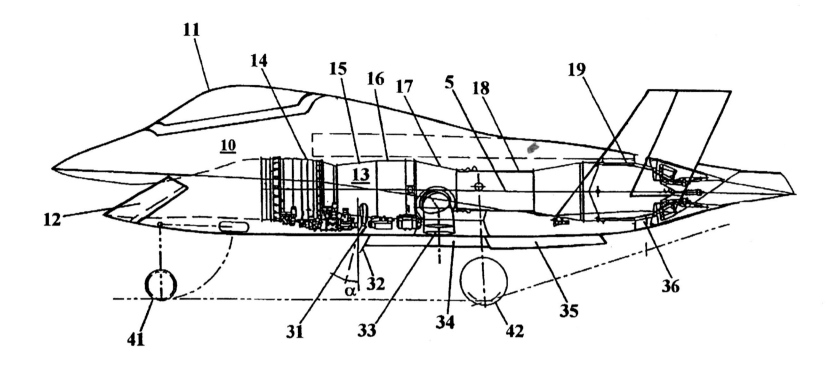

Douglas was relying on an untried control system and a paper lift engine; Lockheed Martin had ground-tested its powered-lift system, and the aerodynamic and stealth features of its design were based solidly on F-22 data.

The evaluators indeed followed this logic. Defense Secretary Bill Perry announced that Boeing and Lockheed Martin would build JSF prototypes and compete to build the production aircraft.

The decision, which would not have occurred if Boeing's stubborn engineers refused to take backseat in a teaming agreement with Lockheed, caused shock in St. Louis,

headquarters of the McDonnell Douglas company. Only weeks earlier, McDonnell Douglas corporate leaders had concluded that the company's commercial aircraft business was in an irrevocable decline and that no investment in future commercial projects was warranted. The JSF loss meant that the company's share of the military market was also, in the long term, headed downward. Weeks after the JSF announcement, McDonnell Douglas and Boeing disclosed that the two companies had agreed to merge. Not one piece of a flyable aircraft had been produced, but JSF had already made its mark on aerospace history.

Boeing's JAST design was ultra-compact and stealthy with a two-dimensional cruise nozzle embedded in the tail and an inherently low infra-red signature. One big challenge was to suppress the radar signature from the engine face, but Boeing believed that a variable-geometry blocker would solve that problem.
Boeing

CHAPTER 2
THE WAR OF THE X-PLANES

There could not have been a more important or earlier test for the newly formed defense giants, Boeing and Lockheed Martin, than the JSF competition. With the re-election of President Bill Clinton, the Pentagon's warplane plans were unlikely to change and JSF would remain the only program in sight. It was far from clear what, if anything, would be left for the losing team to do. With the Pentagon due to pick a winner at the end of 2000, the competitors had four years to prove that they could provide the best value to the customer.

Lockheed Martin moved quickly to recruit McDonnell Douglas' former teammates, Northrop Gruman and British Aerospace, onto its team. The company had won one of the JSF demonstration contracts on its own but knew that it would need help to win the engineering and manufacturing development (EMD) contract in 2000, particularly in the face of Boeing's and McDonnell Douglas' combined resources.

Lockheed Martin's program would be run from Fort Worth, home of the F-16, but the prototypes would be built by the Skunk Works at Palmdale, California. The Skunk Works would also be responsible for building a full-size radar cross-section model for tests at Lockheed Martin's newly upgraded RCS range at Helendale, also in the California desert.

In 1996, Northrop Grumman acquired Westinghouse, which had supplied radars for all of Fort Worth's F-16s and had previously picked up Norden, a company with unique expertise in advanced air-to-ground radars. Northrop Grumman would be the prime sensor supplier to the Lockheed Martin team. In 1997, Lockheed Martin attempted to acquire Northrop Grumman, but the Pentagon's appetite for consolidation was slaked, and the merger was disapproved.

Boeing's JSF organization was based on companies newly acquired by Boeing in its effort to expand out of its core commercial-airplane business. The program head-quarters would remain in the company's high-security building at Boeing Field in Seattle. The Phantom Works in St. Louis, however, would contribute its expertise in manufacturing technology and building prototype aircraft and cockpit designs. Final assembly and flight test would take place a few hundred yards from Skunk Works in a former Rockwell building at Palmdale. Raytheon joined the group as the main sensor supplier.

Churchill once described Lord Jellicoe, admiral of the British Home Fleet in World War I, as "the only man who could lose the war in an afternoon." The leaders of Boeing and Lockheed Martin knew that the same was true of their JSF program managers. Both companies brought new leaders into their programs after winning the demonstration contracts.

Frank Statkus, a 25-year Boeing veteran, took over the company's JSF program in August 1997. He had previously been vice president and general manager for Boeing's military aircraft, including the company's share of the F-22 program. Before that, Statkus had been Boeing's program manager for the F-22—succeeding Dick Hardy, the tenacious architect of Boeing's return to the fighter business and Boeing's program manager on the B-2 bomber.

Lockheed Martin's Frank Cappuccio spent most of his career in the shadow world of secret programs. He joined the Lockheed Skunk Works in 1979 as director of advanced programs, and he left in 1990 to help start Martin-Marietta's even more spooky advanced development operations (ADO) unit in San Diego. He returned to Lockheed Martin and reached the position of vice president of programs and

Lockheed Martin's JSF design settled into a near-final configuration quickly. Key features: the lift fan, three-bearing swivel nozzle at the rear, and diverterless inlets.
Lockheed Martin

Early Lockheed Martin artist's concept shows the Royal Navy JSF launching an MBDA ASRAAM missile. This version features folding outer wings that would have allowed the airplane to fit on the Invincible-class ships; this requirement has been changed and the outer wings are fixed. Lockheed Martin

The original, delta-winged Boeing JSF design roars off the deck of Invincible. The airplane was designed to take off without afterburning using its retractable vectoring nozzles for a Harrier-type STO departure. The aft nozzle would be opened once the airplane was in up-and-away flight. Boeing

technology for the company's aeronautics sector before being placed in charge of JSF.

On the government side, the JSF program office had formed in Crystal City, a complex of offices near the Pentagon that was largely occupied by military tenants. Leadership of the program rotated among the three services with preference to the air force and navy. As the JSF project got under way, Rear Admiral Craig Steidle was in office as the first navy director of the JSF office.

The government program managers stressed repeatedly that JSF was in no way a "fly-off" competition, which was true in two important respects. First, little credit was given for beating the specification in higher speed, greater range, or superior maneuverability. The prototypes—known as concept demonstration aircraft (CDAs)— had three principal tasks: prove the design's "up-and-away" performance characteristics; demonstrate the low-speed performance required for carrier landings; and show that the STOVL concept worked.

Secondly, JSF was not, strictly speaking, a fly-off because two other major elements were in the program. While building and testing the CDAs, each team would design a preferred weapon system concept (PWSC). The PWSC included the design of an operational JSF, detailed proposals for production and support, and a plan for EMD. Large-scale models would be built for stealth tests. The teams would also work on a variety of technology programs. Some elements of this work pre-dated JAST. For instance, the joint integrated subsystems technology (J/IST) demonstration had its roots in USAF research of electrical actuation for flight controls. Others, including much of the avionics activity, were launched in the early days of JAST when it was realized that their effect on cost was decisive.

The CDA designs were not necessarily representative of the final PWSC, because the

requirements themselves were fully expected to change before 2000. The JSF acquisition plan made it clear that the performance targets, on which the CDA designs were based, were not final. It laid out a process by which the service customers would look at the progress of the CDA designs, the different technology programs and the evolving threat, and produce a series of joint interim requirements documents (JIRDs).

In earlier programs, the customer had set the requirement, the contractor had tried to meet it, and the cost was a by-product of this process. This was often the root of cost overruns, when a specific requirement turned out to be harder to attain than expected. For example, an immense amount of effort in the F-111 program had been expended on tweaking, redesigning, and testing the engine inlets so the airplane could reach its Mach 2.5 design maximum speed, which it almost never did in service because low-level bombers don't need to do that.

JSF inverted this process. The cost could and would be controlled independently, and the contractor and customer would agree on what could be designed and built for the money. A cardinal rule was that the cost of changes to

Boeing's STOVL design in a ski-jump departure. Vertical tails are toed-in to help rotate the airplane nose-up, even with the flap/elevon surfaces drooped to boost lift. Draggy, yes—but the Boeing airplane had enormous thrust for take-off, even without afterburners. Boeing

the requirements had to be fully evaluated. If changes resulted in a cost increase, an equal savings had to be found somewhere else. This process was to be formalized in a series of JIRDs and was issued annually.

The JSF office was equally focused on controlling risk. Some people and institutions throughout the government and industry saw JSF as the ideal platform for their pet technologies: new materials, advanced stealth technologies, and new engines. If the JSF program could not afford to demonstrate them before the final choice of a winning design, they were not allowed in the door.

JIRD I was produced in 1995 and focused on size, speed, and stealth; the factors that determine the airplane's shape. JIRD II, issued in June 1997, looked at major trades between performance, cost, and supportability. JIRD III, released in the fall of 1998, addressed a range of issues including supportable stealth technology, adverse

weather, night capability, and mission planning. These led to the final joint operational requirements document (JORD), released in December 1999.

It was therefore quite likely that the CDA and PWSC would be different in major respects. The CDA, therefore, wasn't a prototype. It was proof that the contractor knew how to build the production aircraft. The program office wanted to see that the CDA performed the way that the contractor had predicted. This showed that the engineers understood the design process, the computer codes by which they plotted the airflow around the airplane and the loads on its different components.

The preliminary requirement to which the CDAs were designed was underpinned by three basic concepts. The first was the assumption that other aircraft would take care of the most severe air-to-air threats. The USAF and U.S. Navy did not require JSF to be their primary air-to-air fighter, did not

need to pay for such a capability, and did not want JSF to be perceived as an alternative to the F-22 or Super Hornet.

The requirement was 70 percent weighted towards air-to-ground missions. The Lockheed Martin X-35, for instance, had a higher wing loading than the F-22 and no in-flight vectored thrust, both of which would limit its agility. Supersonic cruise was not required. The JSF's standard AAM would not be the AIM-9X Sidewinder, but the AIM-120 advanced medium range air-to-air missile (AMRAAM), better for self-defense than for dogfighting.

The second principle of the JSF requirement was first-day stealth. This was a post-Cold War concept founded on experience in the first Gulf War, where the threat to coalition aircraft declined rapidly after the first night's operations had damaged Iraqi air defenses. The first-day missions are performed in a stealthy configuration, with a small load of internal weapons; later, the aircraft would carry a heavier load of weapons externally, in order to attack a larger number of targets. Both JSF designs could carry more than twice as much ordnance under their wings as would fit in their weapon bays.

The third key concept was that the Pentagon expected to have retired most of its dumb bombs by the time JSF entered service. By 1996, development of the joint direct attack munition (JDAM) low-cost guided bomb was well under way and it was promising to beat its cost targets. The result was that a small weapon load on JSF would be as effective as a much larger load of unguided weapons.

The most basic JSF requirements of 1996 did not change appreciably through the JIRD process. All three services required an internal load of two JDAMs and two AMRAAMs; the USMC was initially ready to accept the smaller 1,000-pound weapon. The USMC and USAF required an unrefuelled radius of 500 miles and a desired range of 600 miles, but the navy required 600 miles as a minimum. All three required speed and maneuverability "comparable" to current fighters, without rigidly specifying numbers; the USAF had an internal goal of Mach 1.5, but maximum Mach did not have to be demonstrated in the CDA stage.

Stealth requirements varied from one service to another, and did not finally settle down until late in the program.

The highly modified F-16 VISTA research aircraft—equipped with a special flight control system that allows it to replicated different airplanes—was used to evaluate the up-and-away handling qualities of Lockheed Martin's JSF design. Lockheed Martin

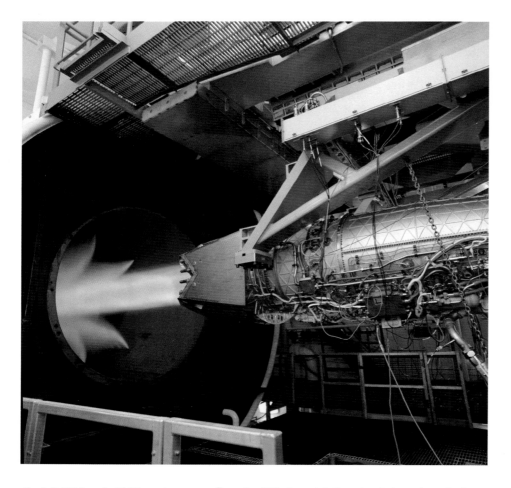

Pratt & Whitney's F119 engine, developed for the F/A-22, was chosen as the basis for the JSF engines. It has a much larger core (high-pressure compressor, combustor and turbine) than the F100 and F110 used on today's fighters, and the modified versions for the JSF could deliver almost 30,000 pounds of thrust without afterburning. Pratt & Whitney

From the CDA viewpoint, though, what was important was to demonstrate that the designs had the potential to reach a very low level of RCS with the help of radar absorbent material (RAM) and other features.

The most basic conflict pitted the marine/RN STOVL requirement against the navy's weapon load and mission radius. The STOVL version needed to land vertically at the end of its mission, with reserve fuel and unused weapons. This limited its empty weight to a proportion of engine thrust, which in turn was limited by the power of a derivative F119, and drove the designer to the smallest, lightest possible aircraft. But the navy aircraft needed to carry a heavy load of weapons and fuel, and a big wing for carrier approaches, together with the extra structural strength required to withstand the shock of catapult

launches and arrested landings. Advanced, exotic technology, like the GE/Allison variable-cycle engine, might do the job but was ruled out by the schedule and the target price: $28 million in 1995 for the USAF, $30 million to $35 million for the USMC, and $31 million to $38 million for the U.S. Navy.

Despite the program office's frequent statements to the contrary, there was one important aspect in which the CDA effort was a fly-off: although a superior CDA might not guarantee a win, a non-performing CDA could guarantee a loss. While there were no, or at least limited, prizes for exceeding the basic "threshold" requirements, there was little doubt that if one team failed to meet the requirement, and the other did not, it would be decisive.

The CDA designs, therefore, were crucial. They were also fundamentally different.

The JSF office avoided using "YF" designations to emphasize that there was no "fly-off," so the CDAs were designated in the X-series, in alphabetical order. Boeing's JSF became the X-32, re-using the CALF designation, and the Lockheed Martin aircraft was the X-35. Both team's CDA prototypes were powered by modified versions of the Pratt & Whitney F119 engines—a selection made by default, because the F119 was the only flight-rated engine with enough power to do the job.

The two were different in the design of the lift system, and this in turn reflected the starting points of the two designs.

Lockheed Martin was one of the first teams to have become involved in the DARPA ASTOVL program, and its follow-on, CALF. Indeed, the ASTOVL program itself had been inspired to some extent by the promise of Paul Bevilaqua's shaft-driven lift-fan.

The challenge in ASTOVL was to develop enough thrust to support the airplane's landing weight and direct the thrust vector vertically through its center of gravity, while keeping the jet velocity and temperature within reason and avoiding problems such as hot-gas ingestion. The SDLF addressed this problem by increasing the power plant's bypass ratio in vertical flight, moving twice as much air at a lower average velocity while using a driveshaft to transfer much of the engine's total energy to a point ahead of the center of gravity.

The X-35's lift/cruise F119 engine was fitted with a "three-bearing" vectoring nozzle: based on a 1960s design, the tailpipe incorporated two angled segments connected by rotating bearings. When the segments rotated in opposite directions the entire tailpipe bent through 100 degrees, providing a small degree of reverse thrust. By adjusting the segments, the tailpipe could also move from side to side.

A clutch on the front of the engine linked the low-pressure spool to a driveshaft. The front end of the driveshaft was permanently connected via bevel gears to the two counter-rotating stages of the lift fan. At full power, the fan would generate 18,000 pounds of thrust and boost the system's total thrust by 44 percent. The fan had a folding nozzle which could direct its thrust up to 60 degrees aft during transition. In vertical flight, the exhaust from the engine's own fan was fed to lateral "roll ducts" which terminated in vertical nozzles beneath the wing roots.

An advantage of this system was that pitch and roll control could be accomplished by transferring energy

Prototype Pratt & Whitney F135 engine for the JSF is prepared for tests. With a larger fan than the F119, it produces more thrust and uses less fuel at subsonic speeds, but is less efficient (and heavier, and has more drag) above Mach 1. Unlike the F/A-22, the JSF is not required to supercruise. Pratt & Whitney

Boeing's forward-mounted engine meant that the inlet had to change section dramatically between the "smiley" lip and the circular compressor face. The shape was designed using computational fluid dynamics (CFD) and constructed using fiber placement. Here, a Viper machine lays fiber on the duct, using heat lamps to cure the material. Boeing

The X-32 forward fuselage was an integrated structure incorporating the cockpit—the aft cockpit bulk-head is white—and the inlet duct, supported by high-speed-machined aluminum frames. Boeing

among the four lift "posts," rather than by bleeding air and power from the engine to a dedicated control system. For roll control, valves feeding the roll ducts would open and close differentially. In the pitch axis, energy could be switched between the aft nozzle and the fan by opening or closing the main exhaust nozzle area and the inlet guide vanes on the fan. Finally, the airplane could be controlled in yaw by moving the aft nozzle from side to side. Total thrust and efficiency remained unchanged and the system promised to be powerful and responsive, potentially solving the Harrier's safety problems.

Another advantage foreseen by Bevilaqua was that the hot exhaust stayed well to the rear of the airplane. Moreover, the cool air flowing out of the fan would tend to keep it there, and away from the engine and lift-fan inlets, reducing the hot-gas ingestion problem.

With ample power in vertical flight, Lockheed Martin could afford to build an airplane that was, in other respects, quite conventional. It strongly resembled the F-22. Lockheed Martin knew that the F-22 was the USAF's top-priority program, so such a resemblance would help keep the

project sold to the largest single customer. The basic air-frame was sized to meet USMC range requirements in its STOVL mode; the navy and air force versions had much greater range because a large fuel tank replaced the lift fan.

The primary risk area for Lockheed Martin was the complex and coupled nature of the powered lift and control system. It included large and highly loaded mechanical components: the clutch and the shaft handled the sort of power usually associated with warships. Fortunately, the shaft ran much faster and therefore did not carry as much torque. Large doors covering the lift/cruise nozzle and the fan inlet and exhaust had to open and close for each flight. If they did not close properly, the airplane would not be stealthy. And, if they did not open, it could not land ver-tically. One unkind engineer nicknamed the Lockheed design "Chitty Chitty Bang Bang," because its fold-out lifting devices reminded him of the flying car in the 1960s movie. The control system would have to modulate thrust accurately for a controlled vertical descent, while handling changes in torque and airflow between the lift fan and the main engine, and would also have to be integrated tightly into the flight control system to ensure a smooth transition between wingborne and jetborne flight.

Boeing had started from a completely different point. The company had not set out to design a STOVL fighter, but reached a conclusion that a common, three-service fighter

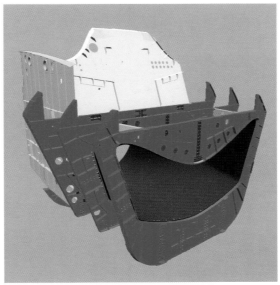

Computer-aided engineering rendering of the X-32 inlet and cockpit structure. This would have been common to all three JSF versions and was attached to the front of the one-piece wing. Boeing

FAR LEFT: Complete Boeing inlet duct, fabricated in one piece—the size of the inlet reflects the 400 pound per second of airflow into the fighter's engine. Computer-aided engineering and fabrication made it possible to build such large and complex components with reasonable reliability. Boeing

was the only way to make the airplane affordable. "Cost was at the head of the line from day one," program director Micky Michellich said in 1995. "And we threw away the book on how we design and build aircraft."

Boeing quickly dismissed any STOVL concept, other than a single-engine direct lift aircraft, as too expensive. This imposed a hard limit on empty weight, even with the most powerful off-the-shelf engine. Because the new fighter would operate alongside the F/A-18 and F-22, "the major threat was the integrated air defense system," according to the program's director of affordability, David Brower. The rear-aspect RCS was particularly important: "Unlike the F-22, we can't run away."

The company was convinced, too, that data-links would be vital to future air combat and that fighters would work in constant touch with each other and with manned and unmanned surveillance aircraft. A decade later, this would be called "network-centric warfare," and would be the centerpiece of defense transformation. One benefit of this approach was that it could ease requirements for onboard sensors; for example, the radar's maximum range might be less and the antenna could be smaller.

The company's first conceptual design was defined as lightweight, stealth, large internal fuel capacity, which gave small airplanes an excellent range. Known as AVX-70, it looked unlike any previous fighter design. To all intents and purposes a flying wing, the fighter's primary load-bearing structure comprised a thick delta wing, built in one piece from tip to tip, with a leading-edge sweep of 55 degrees. Because of that high sweep angle, the wing could be made relatively thick without incurring too much drag in the critical zone around Mach 1. Consequently, the wing could hold 18,000 pounds of fuel, more than twice an F-16's internal fuel load, and it could house antennas in the leading edge.

The cockpit was perched above the apex of the wing and the vertical tails were attached to the wingtips. The engine was attached to the underside of the wing, housed in a long nacelle that also accommodated side-opening weapon bays. The weapons were carried on swing-out racks and terminated in a flattened, pitch-only vectoring nozzle.

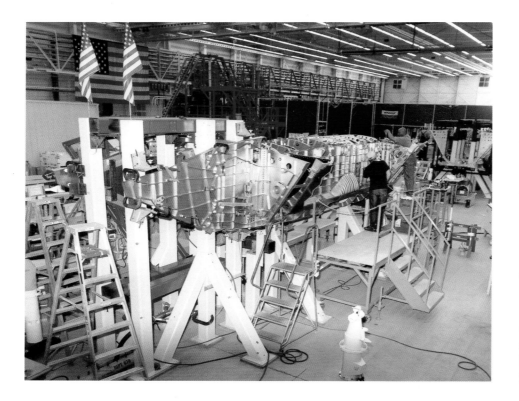

When Boeing issued the first artist's concepts of the AVX-70 the company was coy about some details; in particular, the way in which the designers planned to deliver vertical thrust through the center of gravity. "We'll reveal it when we win," Michellich said. Rolls-Royce and McDonnell Douglas thought that Boeing had borrowed their REX, (remote exhaust) concept, with a blocker in the tailpipe and ducts to bring the gas flow forward, to midship-mounted vectoring nozzles. But Boeing's approach was even simpler. Unlike any jet fighter since the 1940s, the AVX-70 carried its engine forward of the center of gravity with the fan face just behind the cockpit. A straight duct ran from the turbine exit to the augmentor and cruise nozzle in the tail. In the STOVL version, part of the straight duct was replaced by a lift module, incorporating two retractable vectoring nozzles, and a blocker was built into the exhaust.

Folding a delta wing is difficult, because the fold joint is long and deep. A delta could fit in the same deck spot area as an F-18 without folding the wings, as long as the overall length was kept small. But with the engine in the front of the aircraft, conventional bifurcated inlets would add several feet to the overall length, so Boeing selected a radical forward-swept chin inlet.

It was an almost brutally simple layout. One of its chief merits was that most of the differences between the three versions were confined to the underwing nacelle: the STOVL version's nozzle and the reinforced keel that would absorb catapult and arrest loads on the navy version, together with a carrier-type nose landing gear and arrester hook.

Three basic features reduced the Boeing design's RCS in critical directions, according to Brower: a high degree of leading-edge sweep, an after-body design with a two-dimensional exhaust smoothly blended into the rear of the vehicle, and side-mounted weapon bays so that the fighter could release weapons on the side less exposed to a threat radar.

Boeing's JSF was intended to have a very low infra-red signature. In order to provide enough thrust for vertical landing, Boeing's

Boeing's design featured an underwing nacelle that accommodated the engine and the side-mounted weapon bays. It was fabricated from large monolithic, integrally stiffened aluminum panels produced with the help of high-speed machining. Boeing

X-32A forward fuselage, structurally complete at St. Louis and ready for shipping to the final assembly plant at Palmdale. The aluminum substructure has been covered with a carbon fiber skin. Boeing

One of the most challenging components on the X-32 was the one-piece wing skin. The company did not succeed in forming this part from thermoplastic-matrix composites and had to revert to familiar "thermoset" materials. Boeing

The upper and lower wing skins were attached to the substructure in the vertical position. Computer-aided engineering ensured that these very large components fit accurately on the first attempt. Boeing

aircraft had an enlarged fan stage on its engine and a high engine mass flow. The airplane had a great deal of thrust and low drag and normally cruised at partial power. The result was a cool exhaust, which mixed thoroughly in the long exhaust duct behind the engine.

The original AVX-70 had an operating empty weight close to that of an F-16, about 18,500 pounds; a near-stock F119 engine; and internal space for two AMRAAMs or other small weapons. JAST called for a much larger internal weapons bay and a full suite of sensors, and the navy's CV version was required to land aboard the carrier with a heavy weapon load. This drove the size and thrust upwards. The wingtip fins were moved to the aft fuselage, the USAF and navy versions acquired extended wingtips, and the engine was modified with a larger fan.

There were some predictable risk areas in the Boeing design. The powered-lift system was not quite as simple as it looked: not only did it require the usual "puffers" for control, but it incorporated a novel jet-screen nozzle under the forward fuselage, designed to produce a fan-shaped

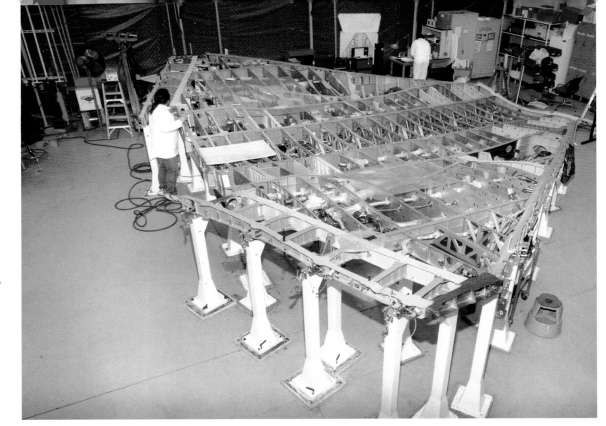

The wing substructure on the X-32s was made from aluminum and titanium. Most of the loads were carried by the composite skins: note that the metal structure is light with many open-work trusses. The white pillars that support the structure in assembly are adjustable and computer-controlled according to laser measurements, making it possible to assemble the wing without heavy fixed tools. Boeing

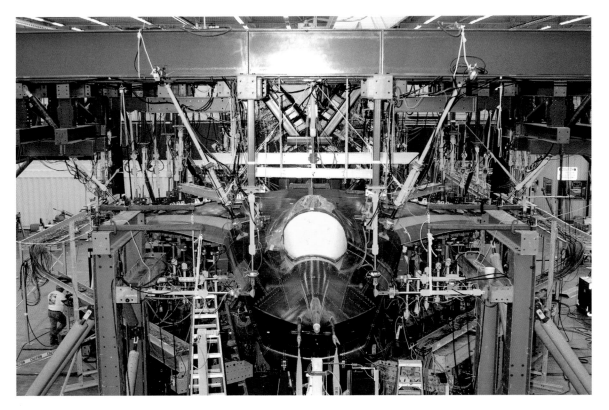

The completed X-32A airframe undergoes structural testing in Palmdale. Tests were necessary because the prototypes were intended to demonstrate vertical landing—unlike other prototypes—therefore, they could not be "over-designed" regardless of weight. Boeing

Joint Strike Fighter

JSF

curtain of high-velocity air that would prevent the hot exhaust gas from flowing into the inlet.

The inlet itself was challenging. The duct was short and tightly curved, for stealth reasons. It partially blocked the line-of-sight from the inlet to the fan face and ensured that radar signals bouncing off the engine would have to bounce off the RAM-coated duct walls before escaping. This alone would not meet RCS targets, so the front of the engine was fitted with a variable-angle set of blocker vanes which would close in cruising flight for maximum stealth, and open for maximum performance for take-off and landing.

The duct section changed dramatically in its short length, from the stealth-aligned sharp-edged inlet lips to the circular compressor face. On the STOVL version, the entire inlet lip slid forward like a jawbone, creating a round-lipped slot to boost airflow at low speeds. Tests and computer analysis said that it would work, but no inlet like it had ever functioned properly; even the simpler Harrier inlet had been a headache in both the original and Harrier II versions.

The delta wing with no horizontal tail was familiar on land-based fighters, but only one such airplane had ever been used operationally by the U.S. Navy: the Douglas

With the wing in place, the X-32A is ready for final fitting-out and assembly with avionics being installed in the nose bays.
Boeing

It looks like an airplane: the X-32A is ready to sit on its wheels, with secondary structure and the vertical tails installed. The main landing gear legs were actually external to the wing structure, retracting forwards with the wheels just behind the leading edge. Boeing

F4D Skyray, which had served for only eight years. There were three basic problems: deltas, like other highly swept wings, tended to assume nose-high attitudes at low speeds, which was bad for over-the-nose visibility; without a horizontal tail, there was no normal way to install lift-boosting flaps; and the trailing-edge elevons had to do double duty for pitch and roll control, making it hard to provide the instant control response that carrier landings demand.

To alleviate these problems, the navy version of the Boeing JSF design used a unique "vortex flap" above the inboard leading edge. Derived from NASA-sponsored supersonic transport research and tested on an F-106B fighter in the late 1980s, the flap was inset into the upper wing skin, was hinged at its trailing edge, and opened upwards, trapping the leading-edge vortex above the wing root. It boosted lift and tended to rotate the airplane nose-up, in turn making it possible to droop the trailing edge on approach.

With simple tooling and accurately assembled components, Boeing was able to assemble both X-32s in parallel with a small team at Palmdale. Music played constantly in this area to drown any voices from the other side of a screen that divided the hangar; the project on the other side was, and remains, classified. Boeing

The size of the X-32's engine—bigger than that of the Lockheed design—is apparent in this view of the completed X-32A being moved to static tests, because of the subway-like tunnel down the nacelle. Also visible here are the overwing vortex flaps. Boeing

Weight was absolutely critical to Boeing. If the airplane was too heavy to land vertically, the designers had few options. Modifying the engine with higher-temperature materials and turning up the thrust would worsen hot-gas recirculation problems; the system already had a hotter exhaust than Lockheed Martin's approach. The engine was about as large in diameter and mass flow as the inlet and the configuration could stand.

Boeing planned to use new materials to reduce weight and cost. Since their ATF studies in the early 1980s, Boeing's fighter team had been apostles for new composite materials using a thermoplastic matrix. Most composites are made from high-tensile-strength fibers embedded in an epoxy-resin matrix material that bonds the fibers together into a rigid component. The epoxy is called a "thermoset" material because when heated, it undergoes an

irreversible chemical reaction which causes it to set hard. Thermoplastics, by contrast, can be re-heated and reformed over and over again. Thermoplastic parts can be built individually and welded together, eliminating fasteners.

Dick Hardy, who founded Boeing's ATF effort, once joked that he'd been accused of trying to build airplanes out of Tupperware—he believed that thermoplastics were the

path to low-cost composite components. But by 1996, there still wasn't a lot of real-world experience with the new materials.

There was one other problem with the Boeing design, and while there were arguments as to whether it mattered, it certainly wasn't a positive. With its thick, blunt wing, minuscule nose and hippopotamus-mouth inlet, the X-32's

A dummy passenger qualifies for his Martin-Baker tie, ejecting from an X-32 cockpit mock-up on the legendary British company's rocket-sled track at Langford Lodge in Northern Ireland. Boeing

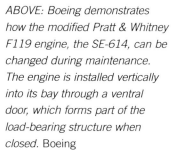

appearance could only be kindly described as functional or distinctive. Fighter competitions are not beauty contests, but combined with the fact that the users associated the Boeing name with commercial jets and bombers, it was another hurdle for Boeing to cover. At the 2001 Paris air show, a Boeing executive finally snapped. "We've run a search on the JORD and we didn't find the word "pretty" anywhere."

Not that there was any time to worry about aesthetics. Although both teams were demonstrating a number of other technologies for JSF in associated programs, the CDAs was the task that would take longest—"the long pole in the tent"—and there was not a lot of time to build a pair of relatively large, densely packed and complex aircraft.

Each team would build two prototype airplanes to demonstrate the three configurations. Both examples of each design could be configured as any of the three versions if necessary, an insurance policy against a mishap in testing. Since Boeing's air force (CTOL) and navy (CV) configurations were externally similar, the first aircraft, designated X-32A, would test both. The STOVL X-32B would be dedicated to powered-lift tests. Lockheed Martin would fly the air force X-35A first, and then fit it with STOVL hardware as the X-35B. The second Lockheed Martin airplane would be the CV X-35C.

The airplanes were required to perform a limited series of tests. The air force version would be used to prove the design's basic handling qualities and explore the flight envelope, including supersonic flight. The navy model would not have to land on a carrier, but would demonstrate simulated carrier approaches at realistic speeds and descent rates, using a carrier-type landing guidance system. The STOVL version would perform short-take-offs and, ultimately, a transition to a vertical landing.

The competing teams would build two other major pieces of test hardware. Powered-lift systems using the same

The X-32 engine was unique in that it was installed in two pieces. The augmentor and final nozzle, linked to the rest of the engine by a simple tubular duct, were slid into place from behind the airplane. Boeing

The first Lockheed Martin X-35, structurally complete at Palmdale. Note the large size of the cavity for the lift engine. Lockheed Martin

mechanical and electronic components as the prototypes would be tested on outdoor test rigs at Pratt & Whitney's alligator-infested plant in West Palm Beach, Florida, and full-scale RCS models, representing the PWSC design rather than the prototypes, would be built and tested.

The competitors were also permitted to add test goals of their own choosing, called "strategic objectives." For example, the program office did not actually require the teams to perform a mission in which the airplane made a short take-off, accelerated to supersonic speed, and then landed vertically, but both elected to do it. Performance in these tests would be compared with "sealed envelope" predictions, previously supplied to the program office. Among other differences, Boeing's X-32A had an operating weapon bay on one side, to show that its unusual weapon stowage system would work.

Another difference between the two teams was that Boeing used the CDA program to demonstrate how its JSF would be built. Reflecting almost a decade of Phantom Works studies and demonstrations, the X-32s exploit a number of manufacturing and assembly innovations.

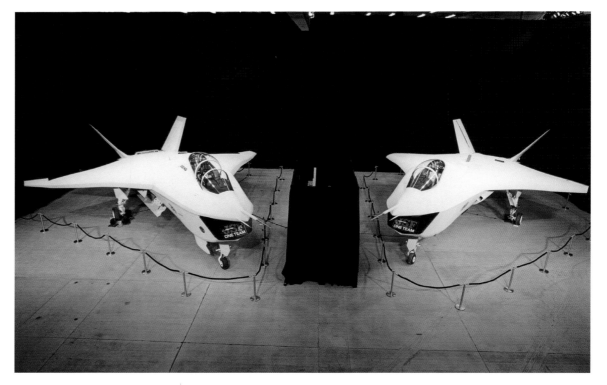

ABOVE: Weight on wheels, the X-35 is ready for structural tests and engine installation. With no engine and no fuel, the landing gear oleos are fully extended and the airplane is sitting higher than normal. Lockheed Martin

ABOVE, RIGHT: The prototype lift fan is ready for testing. The sheer size of the fan—50 inches in diameter—is apparent. A high mass flow boosts the vertical thrust of the entire system and reduces jet velocity, reducing ground erosion. Lockheed Martin

In a theatrical coup at the end of 1999, Boeing unveiled not one, but both X-32s in front of the assembled media and employees at Palmdale. The X-32A, at left, was almost complete, with its engine installed. The X-32B, right, was externally complete but some way from being ready to fly. Boeing

One principle demonstrated in the X-32 program was "design anywhere, build anywhere." This meant the use of computer-aided design and manufacture to fabricate components so accurately that they would fit precisely without shims or trimming. "In the old days," remarked John Priday, leader of the X-32 assembly team at Palmdale, "you allowed half an inch extra on all sides of a skin panel and prayed you had enough. Now, the skins come to us net-trimmed, with zero excess, and they fit like a glove."

One of the new tools used by the X-32 team was a "smart router" for fuel, hydraulic, and oxygen lines. Given the basic outlines of the fighter's plumbing systems, the router defined all the parts in the system in terms of bend radius, wall thickness, junction fittings, and loss factors

working from a deliberately constrained parts library. Such was the confidence in this system that parts arrived at Palmdale with hose brackets already in place.

Both teams had problems. Lockheed Martin ran into delays with the manufacture of the complex prototypes, and overspent its budget with payments to subcontractors. In September 1999, the air force's senior acquisition officer, Darleen Druyun, administered a rigorous dressing-down to Micky Blackwell, the president of Lockheed Martin's aerospace unit. Druyun told Blackwell that Lockheed Martin had lost a major satellite contract, probably the secret Future Imagery Architecture spy-satellite project, because of "crappy design" and, with reference to JSF, said: "If I detect B.S. you go to the bottom of the chart." Blackwell himself was gone by the end of 1999, as part of a restructuring of Lockheed Martin's aerospace activities. The Skunk Works, blamed by senior managers for the cost overruns, lost much of its independence in the process and was placed under the supervision of Fort Worth.

Boeing's prototype thermoplastic wing skins emerged from the autoclave riddled with flaws, and the company was forced to revert to thermoset skins and titanium spars

Lockheed Martin promoted the Skunk Works' credentials on the X-35 program. Here, the first X-35 is posed with (clockwise from left) a U-2R, an SR-71, and an F-117A. The lift fan was invented at the Skunk Works, and the prototypes were built there, but the program was managed from Fort Worth, Texas, home of the F-16. Lockheed Martin

69

At low speed on its first flight, the X-35A looks awkward with its landing gear fully extended and jet nozzle fully closed. The airplane has two small speedbrakes under the rear fuselage, and the rudders are also toed-in to increase drag. Lockheed Martin

Flaperons are lowered at low speeds, increasing lift from the X-35A's basically short, stubby wings. Auxiliary inlets are popped open above the inlet ducts. Lockheed Martin

both for the prototypes the PWSC design. However, the biggest impact was from changing requirements.

Year by year, the JIRD process traded off one requirement against another, within the cost limits established at the start of the program. Stealth targets were adjusted down in 1998 to save money, and raised again in 1999.

Another energetic debate centered on whether JSF would have a gun. The historical record is clear: In the late 1970s, the USAF and other air forces introduced the AIM-9L Sidewinder and similar AAMs, which offered a much wider launch zone around the target than earlier tail-chase weapons. Result: In the Arab-Israeli war of 1973, guns accounted for 70 percent of Israeli kills. In 1982, over the Bekaa valley in Lebanon, 93 percent of the kills were made with missiles; in the Falklands war in the same year, there were no air-to-air gun kills.

Stealth makes gun installations complex, heavy, and expensive. The aperture of a gun barrel has a significant

radar cross-section over a wide angle, peaking in the critical nose-on aspect. On a stealthy aircraft like the F-22, the muzzle is covered by a fast-acting, hydraulically powered door. Quite simply, a STOVL JSF could not afford that much weight and complexity.

Air forces are run not by engineers or cost accountants but by fighter pilots. Like the marines with Guadalcanal, fighter pilots remember how engineers and systems analysts removed guns from fighter aircraft in the 1950s, resulting in near-disaster over Vietnam until the F-4 was hastily modified to carry a gun. The USAF and marines insisted on a gun for JSF; the navy, which regarded the airplane as a bomber with self-defense and was culturally comfortable with a gun-less attack aircraft like the A-6, was less insistent. In 1998, the issue was settled for the time being: the USMC and navy aircraft would be fitted with provisions for a gun pack, and the USAF airplane would have an internal gun.

The most influential requirement was the navy's insistence on a large bring-back payload. By the time JIRD 3 was issued in 1998, the navy had increased its total bring-back weight comprising fuel and weapons from 8,000 pounds to 9,000 pounds and specified an approach speed, which had previously been left to the contractors' discretion.

Lockheed Martin could and did deal with this problem by enlarging the carrier-based JSF's wing, gaining low-speed performance at the expense of transonic acceleration and speed. Boeing's tailless delta was in a more difficult position. The navy requirements drove the size of the

trailing-edge controls upwards, but as Boeing sought to increase pitch authority with larger elevons, the weight of the actuation system became unacceptable. The only answer was to add separate stabilizers and change the wing to a trapezoidal planform.

One attractive option was a novel V-tail designed by Ralph Pelikan, a former McDonnell Douglas aerodynamicist. A skewed hinge-line made it possible for the V-tail to provide pitch, yaw, and roll control. Boeing, with no time for any other problems, went with a less risky four-tail layout. At the same time, Boeing switched to an aft-swept inlet,

Clearing the in-flight refueling envelope was necessary in order to extend test missions; the JSF prototypes did not have as much fuel capacity as the production airplane. The X-35A was equipped to refuel from a USAF tanker, with a boom receptacle above the fuselage. Lockheed Martin

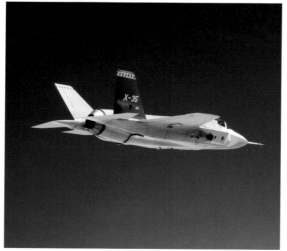

Cleaned up, apart from slightly cracked-open speedbrakes, the X-35A prepares for a high-speed test. Like other tests, the super-sonic run did not aim at a speed target set by the Pentagon, but at "sealed envelope" predictions made by the manufacturer. Lockheed Martin

which was claimed to have better high angle-of-attack performance and improved stealth characteristics. The vortex flaps were eliminated.

It was much too late to make these changes on the X-32s. Boeing engineers argued forcefully that the differences between the X-32 and the new operational design were not as important as they looked. Major characteristics such as the leading-edge sweep and section were unchanged. The changes were not expected to have any great impact on STOVL transition and vertical landing, one of the two most important flight demonstrations.

Boeing pointed out that the CDA and PWSC designs were being developed with the same tools. They started with the same computational fluid dynamics (CFD) software using the "electronic wind tunnel" to estimate the performance

and handling of the initial designs. Then, in the real wind tunnel, they would be evaluated with the same instrumentation and data-processing equipment. This work would form the basis of flight control laws which would be used for the real airplane. The CFD-to-tunnel-to-flight process would be the same for the X-32 and the operational fighter; therefore, Boeing engineers maintained, successful tests of the X-32 would prove that the four-tailed production airplane would fly as predicted. "We have discussed this with the program office, and they believe us," Frank Statkus said in late 1999. "They are satisfied."

In the fall of 1999, Boeing showed its near-final Configuration 374 to the program office. The changes had done nothing for the airplane's looks, particularly in the STOVL version: its wingspan had been clipped to 30 feet to save weight, so that barely 10 feet of wing protruded on each side of the body, ending in a thick stump. The navy and USAF versions had another three feet of wing on each side.

The X-35C made its first flight on December 16, 2000. Both X-35s had the same basic wing structure, surrounded by a "picture-frame" structure which carried the moving wing surfaces. The latter structure was larger on the X-35C, increasing its wing span and area.
Lockheed Martin

The X-35A on approach to landing. The fighter's handling proved to be viceless—to the extent to which the envelope was explored—with good acceleration thanks to the powerful engine and low drag. Lockheed Martin

The X-35C climbs at high altitude for a supersonic test run. The tailhook is visible, although arrested landings were not required. Lockheed Martin

The X-35C had larger horizontal stabilizers than the X-35A/B, intersecting the trailing edge of the wing flaps. It also had separate ailerons for roll control, allowing the flaps to be used to boost lift on approach. Lockheed Martin

The Boeing JSF might not look like a supersonic fighter, but its performance equation combined enormous engine thrust; the fighter's modified and re-fanned F119 would deliver almost 34,000 pounds of thrust without reheat—equivalent to the maximum augmented thrust of an F/A-18, with a low empty weight. The airplane would barely ever need to carry drop tanks and would carry its weapons internally, reducing drag. The Boeing JSF would have much less drag than a conventional fighter carrying an equivalent fuel and weapon load.

Meanwhile, assembly of the X-32s went ahead quickly, once the problems with the wing skins had been bypassed. Every one of the 88 lines in the forward fuselage fit correctly the first time, and there was not a single leak when the X-32A's fuel system was pressure-tested in December 1999, to the open amazement of the Phantom Works' new deputy leader, retired USAF General George Muellner.

At the end of 1999, Boeing presented an impressive piece of theatre in a Palmdale hangar, inviting guests to the unveiling of the first X-32A. Introduced by Tina Turner's "Simply The Best," a tribute to the JSF team, Frank Statkus ordered a black curtain whisked aside to show not one, but two airplanes. Boeing had physically completed the X-32B.

Even though the STOVL airplane was far from ready to fly, it was impressive—particularly since Lockheed Martin's first prototype was still in pieces on the Skunk Works' hangar floor. After the unveiling, Statkus disclosed Boeing plans to end the flight-test program with a single mission, including a short-take-off, supersonic acceleration, and vertical landing.

The X-35A proved easy to handle behind the tanker, clearing its refueling envelope quickly and cleanly. An Edwards KC-135E tanker was used to support flight tests. Lockheed Martin

After Boeing's roll-out, the doors in Palmdale shut. The final JORD had been issued and the contenders were deeply involved in the preparation of their final proposals, a secretive, competition-sensitive activity.

Both teams were breathing hard. By mid-2000, neither prototype had flown. A 40-day engineering strike wiped out most of Boeing's lead. Lockheed Martin was having problems with its clutch in tests at West Palm Beach and was trying to resolve it with changes to the controls. Vibration, oil leaks, and metal shards caused more trouble. In an interview with TV's *Nova*, engineer Scott Winship recalls a team meeting where Lockheed Martin President Dain Hancock warned the lift-fan group that they would lose the competition if they did not get their tests finished on time. Hancock said, "I want to look everybody straight in the eye and ask if you're going to finish this program."

The Pentagon's leaders, up to and including Defense Secretary William Cohen, maintained that the JSF program was making excellent progress and would proceed as planned. Rumor told another story in the most dramatic

The X-35A performs a gentle roll during tests. This view clearly shows the size of the horizontal stabilizers carried on abbreviated booms that jut backwards from the wing roots; the airplane has no aft fuselage to speak of. Lockheed Martin

A slim vortex trails from the wingtip of the X-35A as it flies for the first time above the Mojave Desert. Edward AFB—orginally known as Muroc—has been the center of USAF test flying since the start of the jet age.
Lockheed Martin

The X-35A becomes the X-35B at Palmdale as the team prepares to install the lift fan. Notable features include the complexity of the fan—it includes its own lubrication system and has a row of variable vanes—and the folding "vented-D" nozzle, which was designed to vector nozzle thrust 90 degrees aft. A lighter cascade has replaced it on the production airplane.

versions, one contender had already been declared the winner, leaving the loser to lobby for a minority share of production.

It was a matter of hard fact that the acquisition strategy for JSF was being reviewed, with particular emphasis on the "winner take all" plan conceived in 1996. This was not surprising. Three developments had severely damaged any hopes that the loser in a JSF contest might have a long-term future as an integrator of combat aircraft. Orders for the F-22 and F/A-18 Super Hornet had been cut back in 1997, the export market had remained flat, and the turbulent stock market demanded that any company should abandon any business where it could not see growth and profit.

Since neither Congress nor the Pentagon wanted to see a monopoly in military aircraft, a top-level panel including Cohen and acquisition chief Jacques Gansler was convened in the summer of 2000 to devise ways in which the baby might be hacked in two. . . .

Congress and the General Accounting Office weighed into the fray on the advice of the GAO, which believed that there would still be major technical risks. At the point where EMD was supposed to start, Congress moved to delay an

Lockheed Martin installed a hover pit—lined with heat-resistant concrete and covered by a steel grating—for ground tests of the X-35B. Normally, the powered-lift system would not run at full power close to the ground except transiently, during the touchdown. The pit made it possible to run the system without overheating. Lockheed Martin

With all inlets open and protective covers over the wheels, the X-35B prepares to exercise its lift system. Auxiliary inlets over the body are as far as possible from any hot gas and keep the engine running at low forward speeds. Lockheed Martin

EMD decision until 2001. According to some sources, this was done to forestall a Cohen plan to take the EMD decision in its lame-duck period after the November election.

At the end of June, Cohen lobbed the joint strike fighter decision firmly into the lap of the next administration. The decision to keep a winner-takes-all program as the basis for the draft request for proposals was irrelevant. It did not matter what Cohen and acquisition chief Jacques Gansler decided, because the decision would surely be reviewed by whoever was in the Pentagon when the time came to sign a contract.

More important than the actual announcement were some of the comments that accompanied it. Gansler acknowledged that Boeing and Lockheed Martin did not expect to demonstrate STOVL before March or April 2001. The original plan had been to complete these tests in the winter of 2000, in time to pick a winner in March 2001. Gansler also showed a new JSF engineering and manufacturing

Nobody could call the X-32A pretty, but it was certainly more striking than its rather bland rival. Because Boeing's weapon-bay location was unusual—and was in a position where airflow could be energetic, under the wing-body junction—the right-hand bay was installed on the X-32A and equipped for weapon drops. Boeing

X-35B in transition. The lift-cruise nozzle is pointed aft and is keeping the airplane flying on its wings (see vortex). The fan nozzle is extended and pointing aft, and the fan is at the point of being engaged. Once the fan is up to speed, and the thrust is evenly split between the fan and the aft nozzle, both nozzles can be brought to the vertical, slowing the airplane into a jet-borne hover. Lockheed Martin

development (EMD) schedule that could accommodate a slip into the summer of 2001.

Both teams had clearly slipped by several months since late 1999. Gansler mentioned that there was still a chance that one of the contractors would not demonstrate STOVL. The downselect, he said "would be done when we have one or both having demonstrated vertical lift . . . One could self-eliminate if they don't fly. But as we now expect, they will both fly."

Cohen, in a letter to Congressman Jerry Lewis, chairman of the House defense appropriations committee, made the point that "we will ensure that each contractor is provided a full opportunity to demonstrate the benefits of its approach to the JSF, assuming timely availability of each." Decoded, this meant that the EMD decision deadline, although flexible, would not be extended indefinitely to accommodate one team's slip. Cohen continued with an even more significant statement: "Moreover, I can assure you that each contractor team has stated that they are fully committed to exercising this opportunity." This suggested

Vortex flaps up, leading edge flaps down, trailing-edge flaps down, the X-32A makes a simulated carrier approach at Edwards AFB. The device in the foreground simulates a carrier's optical landing guidance system. Boeing

ABOVE, RIGHT: Both JSF teams performed well during flight tests with no mishaps or serious emergencies. The airplanes were reliable and solidly built. Boeing

Part of the idea behind the side-mounted weapon bays was that, if the JSF was close to a hostile radar, it could turn and release weapons on its "shadow" side, away from the radar. A 2,000-pound bomb is just visible above the AMRAAM guided missile; the bomb was carried on swing arms that would ensure that it cleared the airplane when it was released. Boeing

that someone had told Lewis—whose district included Edwards AFB—that one of the competitors was ready to throw in the towel and negotiate a split program.

Entirely lacking from Cohen's and Gansler's comments was any ringing vote of confidence in the success of both prototype programs, even in terms of such benign boilerplate as: "Both teams are making excellent progress and we are looking forward to a choice between two well qualified competitors."

Either team could be the one in deep trouble and it was almost inconceivable that if one team has failed, the other did not know it. Both teams were working on the same airfield. They shopped at the same Target store, attended the same churches, and their kids played on the same baseball teams. But at Britain's Farnborough air show in July, both teams exuded confidence and said that they were within weeks of their first flights.

Boeing was first. The CTOL/CV X-32A made its first flight on September 28 and had made 17 flights by October 24, when a hydraulic problem led to a no-brakes landing on Edwards AFB's dry-lake runway. On the same day in October, Lockheed Martin flew the X-35A, and had logged eight flights by November 6.

Lockheed Martin's X-35A prototype had completed 23 flights by November 20, when both the X-32A and X-35A

were displayed nose-to-nose at Edwards, reaching a maximum speed of Mach 0.98 and an altitude of 34,000 feet. Two days later, it was Lockheed's turn to post a first: the X-35A became the first JSF to go supersonic, reaching Mach 1.05 in the hands of Tom Morgenfeld. It was then returned to Palmdale to be converted into the STOVL X-35B.

Boeing finished basic tests of the X-32A before the end of 2000, completing its carrier-approach tests during the week of December 18. The airplane had demonstrated in-flight refueling qualities for the navy and, on December 21st, exceeded Mach 1 for the first time. In early February, after some tests of the side-mounted weapon bay, Boeing concluded the X-32A tests after 66 flights and 50 flying hours.

Lockheed's second airframe, in X-35C configuration with the navy's bigger wing and tail, made its first flight on December 16. Lockheed Martin had decided to perform

The X-32A rolls out after an early test flight. With no separate speedbrakes, the airplane used toed-in rudder for deceleration. Boeing

The X-32B performs an early inflight transition. The aft nozzle is shut down and the vectoring nozzles are pointed some 45 degrees aft of the vertical. The vectoring nozzles were designed so that they moved from 90 degrees down to the stowed-and-retracted position in one rotating action. Boeing

81

carrier-landing tests at navy's flight-test center at Patuxent River, Maryland, on the grounds that sea-level testing would be more realistic, as most aircraft carrier operations take place at sea level. This meant that a certain amount of flight-testing had to be completed before the airplane could be cleared for the 2,500-mile cross-country flight. The X-35C was ferried to Pax River on February 10 and finished carrier-approach trials a month later.

Both teams, by the end of March, had passed their CV and CTOL trials. STOVL, however, was clearly going to be the critical test. After 220-plus transitions at West Palm Beach, Boeing's STOVL propulsion system was installed in the X-32B in July 2000, and finished its initial ground runs by the end of the year. Lockheed Martin did not install the lift fan in the X-35B until January.

On January 10, Boeing announced that the X-32B had completed its low-to-medium-speed taxi tests and released photos that clearly showed the airplane's unique

The massive inlet had raked lips for reduced RCS. Variable vanes in front of the engine opened for maximum thrust at take-off and landing and closed in flight to block reflections from the engine face. They caused some thrust loss, but the X-32 could afford it. Boeing

An early sign of problems in the Boeing camp: the X-32B emerges for taxi tests with the inlet "jaw" missing, suggesting that there may have been problems with airflow in the slot between the jaw and inlet. Boeing

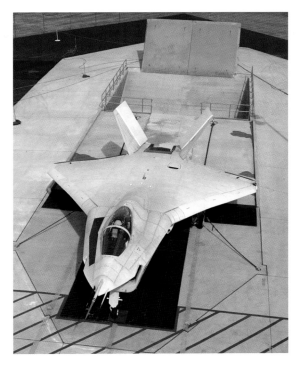

Lockheed Martin started powered STOVL ground-runs at Palmdale late in February. A month later, the system had completed 90 test runs and had repeatedly run to full operational thrust. Lockheed Martin had reason to believe that Boeing's PWSC would need more power than the X-32 and stressed that its prototype engine had delivered as much thrust as its production version would need.

But the X-35B was still firmly on the ground at Palmdale on May 11, when the Boeing X-32B made a cross-country flight to Patuxent River to complete its STOVL tests. The choice was significant, particularly as rival Lockheed Martin planned tests at Edwards. The navy base is 39 feet above sea level; Edwards is at 2,300 feet and daytime temperatures can be 10-15 degrees higher, causing a significant reduction in jet thrust.

As the Paris air show wrapped up in June, Boeing could announce that the X-32B had made a jet-borne landing at 90 knots; four days later it hovered at 200 feet, and on June 27 it made a vertical landing. A short take-off on July 2 completed the government-mandated tests, after 58 flights.

jawbone-like inlet to be missing. It was still absent two months later, when the X-32B performed its first maximum-thrust engine runs at Palmdale. The airplane was tethered to a steel grid above a concrete-lined pit, avoiding hot-gas re-ingestion. The inlet jaw was installed for the first flight in CTOL mode on March 29. By mid-April, the airplane had converted from CTOL to STOVL in flight, an essential preliminary to a vertical landing.

Boeing's complete STOVL engine on test at West Palm Beach, complete with two-dimensional aft nozzle and vectoring nozzles. The aft nozzle also acted as a blocker, preventing exhaust from escaping as butterfly valves opened the vectoring nozzles.
Boeing

But photos showed that not only was the inlet jaw missing, so were the landing gear doors: even at Pax River, the X-32B clearly had not an ounce of thrust to spare. Later, it would emerge that the X-32 was 1,500 pounds overweight and that it could not land vertically with all of its components in place. The weight problem would be eliminated in the PWSC airplane, Boeing promised the Pentagon. And yet something must have happened between the late-1999 rollout and flight test, because Statkus had talked of a supersonic flight and vertical landing; the stripped-down airplane could not accomplish that mission.

Meanwhile, Lockheed Martin rapidly closed the gap, with the help of its 40,000 pounds of vertical thrust. The airplane hovered at Palmdale on June 23, and after a

sequence of "push-up" flights to progressively higher altitudes it was ferried to Edwards. The first mission including a short take-off, transition to wing-borne flight, and a vertical landing took place on July 16. On July 20, Lockheed Martin trumped Boeing by performing a short take-off, supersonic acceleration, and vertical landing; the goal that the X-32B could not reach. The X-32B made a short take-off, went supersonic, and converted to STOVL mode on its 77th and next-to-last flight on July 28, but the actual landing was short, not vertical.

By the end of July, both flight-test programs were complete and data had been submitted to the government, alongside the massive and detailed EMD proposals prepared by both companies. After the frantic pace of flight testing,

and four years of intensive work on the prototypes, the teams had little to do but wait.

Both sides sounded confident in public; the truth was different. The program managers believed Boeing when it said that the changed planform of its PWSC airplane did not involve additional risk, but the program office was not the source selection authority and that view was not universally accepted, as program manager General Michael Hough clearly implied in May 2001. "I'm absolutely confident," he said. "We model nuclear explosions, and you're going to tell me that we can't model performance?" But

Hough went on to acknowledge that some people saw the issue differently. "It's frustrating. It's not hard to get the new thinking in, but we can't get the old thinking out."

Boeing had always been the high-risk, unconventional competitor. Even in the last months before source selection, Statkus continued to talk about the inadequacy of "old ways of doing business." But it meant that Boeing had to do more than just win. Twice, within the span of institutional memory, the USAF has chosen an unconventional solution from a less experienced contractor—General Dynamics' win over Northrop with the F-16, and Northrop's defeat of

In this test, the 2D nozzle has been removed and replaced by a test fixture, and exhaust smoke can be seen coming from the vectoring nozzles and the "jet screen" nozzle ahead of them. Boeing

A media day in late 2000 brought the two JSF prototypes together for the first time; the contrast between the relatively conservative Lockheed design and the more radical Boeing could not be more marked. Bill Sweetman

Tom Burbage, right, was brought in to head Lockheed Martin's JSF program in late 2000; the company was confident, at that point, that it could beat Boeing, and Burbage's job was to maintain support for the entire JSF program. Lockheed Martin

Lockheed/Rockwell with the B-2. In both cases, the winning design was overwhelmingly superior. In order for Boeing to win JSF, either Boeing had to win decisively on cost or on performance, or Lockheed Martin had to fail. By late 2000, with the Lockheed Martin STOVL system finally working properly, it was less and less likely that this would happen.

Boeing missed its own test goals and did not perform a vertical landing with a complete airplane. Given that vertical lift was a known risk area, this shortfall was more

The two JSF designs were very different in shape but quite similar in size. What you might not expect from this view, though, is that it is the aircraft on the left that accommodates more internal fuel. Delta wings are remarkably efficient. Lockheed Martin

The last evening light before the November 2000 media day catches the JSF contenders nose to nose. The light also provides a clear view of the Boeing airplane's unique inlet, in which the underside of the cockpit section forms the upper wall of the duct. Lockheed Martin

than symbolic. It demonstrated that the complete X-32 had a small negative margin of vertical thrust, contrary to Boeing's own predictions. By the late summer of 2001, Boeing's chances in JSF seemed to be receding.

Boeing may have submitted a less expensive bid, but the Pentagon was free to reject it if it believed that the risk was greater. Later, explaining their choice, Pentagon officials repeatedly used the words "best value" rather than "lower cost." This was essential. The JSF contract price would be an estimate. A fixed-price contract would be meaningless, because in five years there would be no alternative to JSF.

The program itself had proved popular with the incoming Bush administration. In fact, JSF during 2001, advocates succeeded in portraying the new fighter as just the kind of "transformational" weapon that the new administration said it wanted: multi-service, stealthy, mobile, and smart.

Carrier-landing requirements drive the switch to four tails. The delta wing could not provide enough control and lift capability to meet the Navy's requirements for bring-back to the carrier without expanding the wing area and control size to an unacceptable degree. Boeing

One program official asked later what made the joint program work; the response was hunger. The services needed fighters and recognized that none of them would get a new airplane unless it was produced jointly. As the final decision date for the JSF drew closer, though, there were some indications that USAF and navy were not enthusiastic about the airplane and believed that they could develop better aircraft in individual programs.

For example, under a highly classified "black" program sponsored by the USAF, Boeing's Phantom Works had tested a demonstrator for an ultra-stealthy attack fighter with no separate tail. Named the *Bird of Prey*, after a Klingon spacecraft in *Star Trek*, the airplane was designed to test a sophisticated illumination system that would make it almost undetectable in daylight. The JSF seemed pedestrian by comparison.

But as independent analyst Terry Mahan pointed out in a trenchant brief in late 2000, the economic case for JSF was cast-iron. Its 4,000-aircraft production run meant that the unit program cost, including research and development was one-third of the price tag for a single-service airplane of which 500 might be built. Some leaders, Mahan pointed out "don't yet understand the magnitude of the difference between JSF and anything else. It's not just more expensive, it's three times more expensive for the same level of capability." If the USAF wanted to add features such as daylight stealth and tailless design, Mahan explained, "the new plane is guaranteed to cost more (with R&D included) than simply buying the same number of additional F-22s."

The administration's first quadrennial defense review, being readied for publication in early September, was in favor of pursuing the competition as planned. The September 11 attacks delayed the JSF decision, but did not affect it. The Pentagon still needed fighters; and if anything, the difficulty

The change to four tails did nothing for the Boeing design's looks. The leading edge shape remained the same, as did the concept of a thick one-piece wing containing all the internal fuel, but the result of the change was a short-coupled, thick-waisted airplane. Boeing

Boeing Joint Strike Fighter	
Conventional Take Off and Landing	
Length:	47' 3.75"
Wingspan:	36' 0"
Height:	13' 3"

The revised STOVL version was a configuration only its mother could love, with brutally cropped wings extending less than ten feet either side of the body. High thrust and low drag—with no external stores—would have given it acceptable performance, Boeing claimed. Boeing

Boeing Joint Strike Fighter	
Short Take Off and Vertical Landing	
Length:	45' 11.5"
Wingspan:	30' 0"
Height:	13' 3"

of securing bases from which to mount the attack on the Taliban underscored the flexibility of the new airplane.

As the decision date drew closer, the tea-leaves read more like a win for Lockheed Martin with each passing week. In September, Bill Lawler, vice president and general manager for business development at Boeing's military aircraft and missile systems division, stopped short of saying that the company would abandon the fighter business outright if it did not win JSF, but commented, "As many people have observed, if you don't have a significant piece of JSF, your ability to maintain a manned fighter infrastructure is questionable."

"JSF," said Lawler, "is one of the pivotal programs that determine the direction of research and development." Developing manned fighters requires a continuing, dedicated investment in flight test facilities, simulators, and the ability to integrate high-performance pilot-rated systems. "And unless you have products that you're building, it's very hard to sustain it. We've seen evidence of that in Russia, and in the fact that the United States is down to two front-line fighter companies." But Lockheed Martin people weren't talking about what would happen if they lost.

Likewise, it was Missouri's Congressional delegation, otherwise known as the Keep Missouri Green movement because of its ruthlessly effective campaigns to suck government money into the state, which first came to Capitol Hill with the idea of splitting the JSF program and granting a share to the losing team. Led by Senator Christopher Bond and Representative Todd Akin, whose district included Boeing's St. Louis plant, the delegation introduced legislation mandating the establishment of a second JSF production line. The line would apply regardless of which company won, they said, but their Texas and California counterparts weren't advocating the same legislation and nobody really believed that the Missourians thought that Boeing was going to win.

One undoubted effect of 9/11 was to intensify the pressure on the Pentagon to open a share of JSF to Boeing. The market for Boeing's commercial jets, which had been softening rapidly since the summer, had tanked horribly after the 9/11 attacks and the company had laid off tens of thousands of workers.

The announcement was set for October 26—as usual, a Friday, after the markets had closed. On Thursday, a senior official in the Office of the Secretary of Defense called the JSF program office. Citing congressional concerns, the OSD official asked the program office to wait three to four months before awarding a formal contract.

But there were people in the JSF office who did not want to wait. Any Boeing JSF work would have to be taken away from the team that had worked to win it, and cutting Boeing in would cost time and money as the program was rearranged; Lockheed Martin's team had worked together for almost five years. When the OSD call came through, somebody in the JSF office called an ally in the U.K. Ministry of Defence, who passed the news to his boss. Within minutes,

The four-tail CV version would still be able to fit on the carrier without folding the outer wings, Boeing claimed. One unusual feature of the design was a twin-wheel nose landing gear that was split just above the wheels: the wheels folded in opposite directions on retraction to lie flat, side-by-side, under the inlet duct. Boeing

The Boeing JSF was designed for easy maintenance. Most of the key equipment was housed in the sides of the lower nacelle, at a convenient height for access. Boeing

Boeing's CV airplane seen turning into a carrier approach. Boeing hoped that its recent experience with carrier-based aircraft—acquired along with McDonnell Douglas—would put it in good stead with the Navy. Boeing

a high-level official in the United Kingdom placed a call to a very senior Pentagon executive. It may have been Britain's defense procurement minister, Lord Willy Bach, a fan of hard-boiled crime fiction, because as a JSF program official puts it, the gist of the call was, "Grow some balls and make a decision." Within 30 minutes of the first call, the decision was reversed. The system development and demonstration (SDD) contracts would be awarded immediately.

Lockheed Martin's JSF program manager Tom Burbage, who had smoothly succeeded Cappuccio in late 2000, recalls that he only heard the first syllable of the company's name at Fort Worth; the rest was drowned out as hundreds of workers cheered as they watched on big-screen TV. In Seattle, a crestfallen Frank Statkus asked Boeing CEO Phil Condit, in Washington, "Is it winner-take-all?" It looked that way, Condit said. "I'm sorry," Statkus told Boeing President Harry Stonecipher.

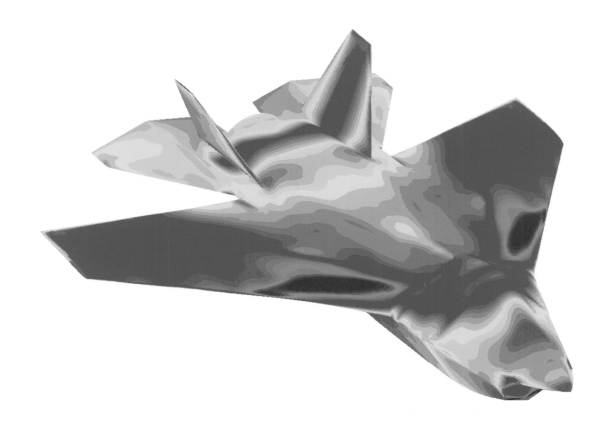

Computational fluid dynamics (CFD) was used extensively in the design of the JSF. Colors correspond to air pressure—red is high, blue is low. Boeing

The lift system of the four-tail airplane was rather more complicated than what was seen in the original patents, with the addition of a bigger jet-screen nozzle and larger "puffer" controls on the nose, just behind the inlets. Boeing

93

A full-scale model of the Boeing JSF design was displayed at the Farnborough air show in the United Kingdom in July 2000. The auxiliary inlets beside the cockpit were for cooling and auxiliary power. The original idea was to put those inlets in the main inlet duct, but with the redesign the main inlet was at its largest practical size. Boeing

Boeing argued that crucial features of the JSF design, including its one-piece wing and the leading-edge shape, did not change with the switch to four tails. This meant that lessons learned from the X-32s could be directly applied to the production airplane. Boeing

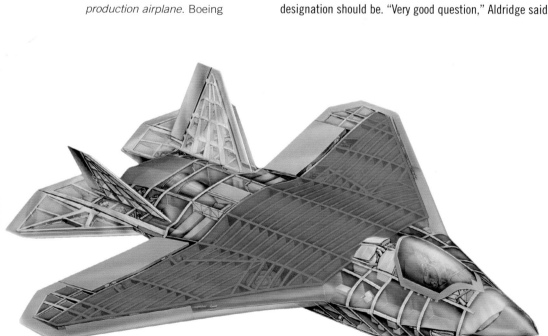

The unexpected move—a gap between announcement and contract award is by no means unusual—wrong-footed Boeing's congressional shock troops. Now, bringing Boeing into the program would mean renegotiating Lockheed Martin's contract. Pentagon Acquisition Chief Pete Aldridge said, "If Lockheed Martin wishes to use the unique talents of Boeing, they are free to do so. We're not forcing them to do it. If they would like to do that, that's up to them." Lockheed Martin Aeronautics President Dain Hancock, meanwhile, said that the company had "a very specific proposal and a signed contract," which could not be changed without government involvement. Any Boeing participation "would have to bring a specific benefit," Hancock said. Translated, that meant that Boeing was out.

Aldridge's press conference announcing the award placed another permanent mark on the program: the wrong designation. The previous fighter in the U.S. designation system was Northrop's YF-23A, so the JSF should have been the F-24, or even the F/A-24, given its air-to-ground bias. At the conference, though, a reporter asked Aldridge what the designation should be. "Very good question," Aldridge said,

but he didn't know the answer. In fact, there was no answer, since no designation had been assigned yet. The Pentagon moderator pitched the question to Program Director General Mike Hough. Momentarily confused, Hough said "X-35." Aldridge misheard him and repeated the designation as "F-35."

This placed the Pentagon in a dilemma: admit a mistake or permit an out-of-sequence designation. The JSF office made its choice in December, officially requesting F-35 under the Mission Design Series on the ground that it was "consistent with the statement made by [Aldridge]." The USAF's nomenclature office forwarded the request to the Directorate of Programs, the final authority, in April 2002, but couldn't resist a peevish paragraph recommending an in-sequence F-24 designation. By that time, though, F-35 had momentum and it was officially confirmed in June 2002.

Like the elimination of McDonnell Douglas in 1996, the choice of Lockheed Martin had a seismic impact on the aerospace industry. The Pentagon did attempt to steer a consolation prize to Boeing in the form of a lucrative, front-loaded contract to lease 100 KC-767 tankers, but it drew intense political opposition. At the end of 2003, Boeing's chief financial officer, Mike Sears, was fired for ethics violations related to the tanker deal. CEO Phil

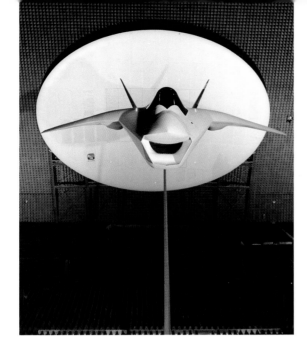

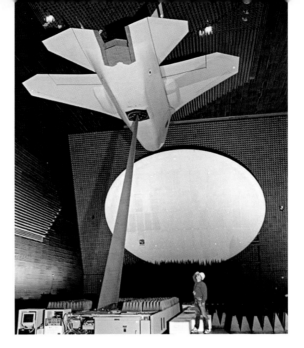

Condit followed him out the door a week later; the failure to win JSF was one of many setbacks that had cast doubt on Condit's strategy of growth through acquisition and expansion into new businesses.

Lockheed Martin had other concerns. Among those who expected a delay between the announcement and a contract award was the company's management. After the announcement, Lockheed Martin leaders convened over the weekend. They had a 126-month, $13 billion contract in hand, and the clock was running.

CHAPTER 3

ONE SIZE FITS ALL

The F-35 is an outwardly conventional design, looking like a smaller and plumper cousin of the F-22. However, it includes new technology aimed at delivering a versatile, high-performance stealth aircraft with an affordable price tag. In many respects, the F-35 is required to deliver F-22-like characteristics at a bargain-basement price, requiring major innovations in design and manufacture.

At the same time, JSF incorporates a remarkable ability to operate safely from small ships and short runways, as well as from carriers and conventional airfields. And, although it is smaller than the F-22, it is expected to carry larger internal weapons.

Any major military aircraft program is a massive enterprise. It is far more than just building an airplane, although the task of designing and testing the "air vehicle" is the single longest and most difficult element of the job. While the aircraft itself is being designed, other teams around the world design all its parts: the radar, the cockpit, the engine, and so on, each of them complex in itself.

At the same time, the production lines that will fabricate the airplane and all its parts are designed and built. Even though production may take place in existing buildings, the tools and machines used in the process will be new. In the case of JSF, with its demanding cost targets, the manufacturing system will use technology that was in its infancy when the F-22 started full-scale development in 1991.

There is no point in building hundreds of aircraft if nobody is trained to fly and fix them. A system to train pilots and maintenance crews—dozens of people for each airplane—must be running smoothly when the aircraft are delivered. Also essential are the logistics and support system that supplies spare parts and tools to the operators.

Airplanes used to be built like boats or ships. The designers started with a basic airframe and engine; detail teams stepped in to decide where cables and fuel lines should run, and to design features like the cockpit and bomb racks. The same logic prevailed in manufacturing: the airframe was put together and "fitters" then installed all the parts.

But as airplanes became more complex and production runs increased into three or four figures, it became clearly apparent that such informality was a recipe for disaster. After a few painful episodes, one might mention the Boeing B-29 Superfortress and the North American F-86D in which airfields ended up lined with expensive airplanes, all useless because they lacked an essential part of modification, the aviation industry invented the concept of systems management—now in use by almost every industry. The key to this was a highly detailed plan under which the airplane, its subsystems, the factories, and the training and logistics system were all designed concurrently, each on its own part of a master schedule.

The goal was that everything should be finished at the same time. If one group of engineers did hit an unexpected problem, the overall program managers would know because that part of the work would fall behind schedule. They could then decide whether to pour extra resources into that area or let the entire program slip.

There are risks to the "concurrency" involved in this approach. For example, the JSF schedule calls for hundreds of airplanes to be on order, in varying stages of manufacture, before tests are finished. The risk is that problems will emerge during flight tests and that those will require fixes that are not easy to implement on an airplane that has

The production F-35 will not be radically different from the X-35A, seen here during flight tests. Maneuverability and acceleration will be similar to that of an F-16C; top speed will be about Mach 1.5, and supercruise—the F/A-22's ability to fly at Mach 1.7 without afterburners—is not a feature of the F-35. Lockheed Martin

The engine of the F-35 is located well forward because the nozzle needs to be close to the center of gravity, and the tails loads are carried by boom-like structures alongside the nozzle. The structure is complicated and has resulted in some weight gain. Lockheed Martin

already been built. For example, in 1991 the B-2 bomber hit problems with its stealth technology, requiring some extensive modifications including a new wing leading edge. Only three of the 21 B-2 bombers were delivered from the factory with those modifications, and the others had to be expensively modified.

But if there were no concurrency, military airplane projects would take even longer than they do, and their time-span is already measured in decades. The F-22 is due, at the time of writing, to enter service in late 2005, more than 14 years after the full-scale development contract was awarded and 19 years after Lockheed and Northrop were selected to build

prototypes. The full-scale development contract for the V-22 tilt-rotor was awarded in 1986, an early version, without the modifications needed to make it readily maintainable in the field, will undergo an operational evaluation in mid-2005.

The F-35 was supposed to do somewhat better than this—nine years from contract award to initial operational capability (IOC)—but we'll see. The schedule has already slipped. In defense of the Pentagon, though, the project is extraordinarily complicated.

There are three different versions, which will all handle differently. The normally arduous flight-test program is bigger than usual, including a carrier-landing program—never a cakewalk —and the first short-take-off, vertical landing test program since the 1980s. There are two different engines. JSF is the vehicle for a new generation of radar technology, and has a cockpit design that was only dreamed of 20 years ago.

As noted in the previous chapter, the Pentagon's leaders moved very quickly to award the system development and demonstration (SDD) contract for JSF and forestall any attempt by Congress to award a share to Boeing. In fact, says Lockheed Martin JSF Vice President Tom Burbage, it was not until the day after the winner was announced, on October 26, that Lockheed Martin realized that the $18.9 billion, 126-month contract had been formally awarded and the schedule clock was ticking.

The SDD JSF design is very close to the designs shown during the concept development phase. It resembles the X-35 more than the F-22 resembled the YF-22, according to Burbage, and wind-tunnel tests before the outer shape was frozen in 2002 looked at refinements and details rather than basic design issues. For example, the camber and twist of the CV version's larger wing were adjusted to provide high lift without the kind of transonic drag issues that afflicted the F/A-18.

Under the SDD phase of the program, the Lockheed Martin team will build 14 flying development aircraft: five USAF aircraft, five navy variants, and four STOVL aircraft. There will be eight non-flying full-size articles: one static-test and one fatigue-test article for each variant, six in all, a signature model, and a carrier-suitability test vehicle.

The first aircraft off the line will be A-1, the first CTOL aircraft, because the CTOL design is the simplest and the

base for the other two versions. Under the original plan, A-1 was due to fly toward the end of 2005, 48 months after contract award. Next in the air is B-1, the first STOVL design. The U.S. Marines and the United Kingdom, with their aging and attrition-prone Harrier fleets, have less leeway than other users to wait for the F-35B. B-1 was originally intended to fly in mid-2006, with the CV variant making its maiden flight at the end of the year. The remaining test aircraft were to join the program at a rate increasing to one aircraft a month.

Software for the JSF will be released in four blocks. Block 0 software will include flight control and basic vehicle management functions, and will be used for initial flight tests and envelope expansion. Block 1 will include all the avionics hardware and will allow for single-ship operation. Block 2 will include multi-ship operation and interoperability with U.S. assets such as Joint STARS and AWACS; this will be the IOC standard for the U.S.

Marine Corps. Block 3 will feature interoperability with the United Kingdom and other European systems and will be the initial operational capability (IOC) standard for the USAF, USN, and United Kingdom.

Weapon clearances will proceed in parallel with the software blocks, but are not directly linked to them. The first weapons to be cleared will be the Boeing GBU-31 joint direct attack munition (JDAM) and AMRAAM, followed by the new Small Diameter Bomb and a range of externally carried weapons.

Oddly, it is the STOVL and navy versions, a minority of the production run, which have defined the basic shape of the F-35. The STOVL version sets the internal layout of the fuselage and CV requirements have driven the wing and tail configuration. From the viewpoint of risk, this was seen as beneficial because it caused the design to resemble the F-22; however, the differences between the F-22 and F-35 have proved significant.

The X-35C performs a roll over Edwards AFB. Note that flaperons, ailerons, and stabilizers are all deflected—like other modern fly-by-wire airplanes, it uses all available "effectors" to achieve whatever effect the pilot has called for. Lockheed Martin

The production F-35 will be cleaner than the prototypes, which did not have to demonstrate stealth technology—that was done with full-scale model in the RCS range. Canopy details will also be different, including a lower sill line. Lockheed Martin

The F-35 and F-22 are the only all-new fighters designed in the last 30 years with a "conventional" four-tail configuration with horizontal and vertical stabilizers. In that time, Europe, China, Israel, and Russia have produced canard (tail-first) designs. The initial CALF/ASTOVL designs were canards; it was a good layout in terms of supersonic drag issues, a forward-mounted lift fan, and the promising F-16U design: a tailless delta.

Structurally, the F-35 and F-22 have a significant common feature: the horizontal tails are not attached to a monolithic rear fuselage but to skeletal tail booms that extend well beyond the exhaust nozzle, rather like an F-4 Phantom. They might as well be deltas, from the viewpoint of structure and mass distribution. However, they are both four-tail designs, for different but compelling reasons.

The F-22 has four tails because it had to meet requirements for both stealth and agility, including controllability over a very wide speed range. The result in a tail-first design would have been awkwardly large canards, rather than big aft stabilizers which, in terms of stealth, could be located in the shadow of the wing.

The F-35 has four tails because it has to land on a carrier. A carrier landing requires precise, responsive control at low airspeeds, which means effective flaps, ailerons, and stabilizers. The U.S. Navy has only flown one delta—the F4D Skyray—and was reluctant to accept a canard, although the Dassault Rafale appears to have proven suitable for operations off the French Navy's relatively small carriers. On a canard, though, drag considerations limit the size of the foreplane; there are no such limits on the aft surface of a four-tail design.

The need to build carrier-based STOVL and CTOL versions with a high degree of commonality provided Lockheed Martin with another reason to choose a four-tail design, with a moderately tapered wing. It was clear that the STOVL and CTOL versions, absent any requirement for outstanding agility, could get by with a smaller wing than the CV variant, saving a great deal of weight. But a delta-type wing, even with an F-22 planform, would be complicated in this respect because increasing the span meant increasing the root chord, dramatically affecting the structure and aerodynamics of the wing-body junction. With the F-35 layout, Lockheed Martin could and did give

X-35C closes on the tanker. Both prototypes were boom-refueled because the objective was to extend test missions and not to evaluate refueling. The F-35B and F-35C will have refueling probes. Lockheed Martin

the CV version a 40 percent larger wing than the STOVL and CTOL aircraft, without major changes to the mold line or internal structure of the fuselage.

The hard fact is, though, that the four-tail layout is not the lightest or most efficient layout for the STOVL or CTOL airplanes. As Lockheed Martin showed with the F-16U design and Boeing demonstrated with the X-32, a delta provides enormous internal fuel capacity. Also, as seen on the Dassault Rafale, it makes it possible to accommodate a huge load of external stores, including semi-conformal air-to-air missiles that do not occupy an underwing pylon and add very little drag.

Without a great deal of volume in the wing, the fuselage has to accommodate the propulsion system, weapons, fuel, and most of the other systems. In this respect, once

again, the F-35 resembles the F-22. Both fighters are laid out in a way that is analogous to a bird, with wings for flight, tails for control, a head or fore-body for thinking and sensing, attached to a central trunk that provides energy and storage.

The trunk or mid-body section is a complex assembly because it accommodates most of the airplane's systems and weapons. It is put together around a series of bulkheads, each made in one piece from a forged or pressed billet of titanium alloy. The bulkheads are pressed as closely as possible to the final shape, "near-net-shape" is the technical term, and then loaded into a computer-controlled machine tool which literally carves the material into its final shape, cutting away as much as 80 percent of the titanium in the process. Lugs drilled into the bulkheads

carry the attach points for the wing spars and main landing gear units, and cut-outs accommodate the engine tunnel, weapon bays, and other equipment runs.

The bulkheads are a good example of the "cousin parts" concept that is used throughout the JSF structure. The classic problem with building a common fighter for the USAF and navy was that the extra strength required for a carrier landing. For instance, a 12-foot-per-second maximum landing impact, equivalent to pushing the airplane off a loading dock, would make the USAF airplane unacceptably heavy. If the structure was redesigned to reduce its weight, the advantages of commonality would disappear.

The solution to this dilemma was to design the airplane so that the structural loads are concentrated in the smallest possible number of components. These parts are built in three versions which carry different loads but look basically the same; they are made from the same materials on the same forging and milling tools, and are assembled in the same way, but the tool leaves more metal on the CV components. For example, the wing lugs on the Navy version are larger, to accommodate the larger wing, but there are the same number of lugs and the pins that hold the wing spars to the bulkheads are in the same place. The forward bulkhead members of the STOVL version have an aperture

for the fan driveshaft, but are otherwise similar to the CTOL airplane.

The goal is to reduce or eliminate "scar weight," which is the extra weight of a component that is needed to withstand CV loads but is still carried on the CTOL and STOVL versions, without sacrificing too much commonality. It is a complex process, in which simplicity and commonality, and hence cost, must be traded against weight and is greatly facilitated by computer-aided design tools.

In fact, much credit for the cousin-parts discipline belongs to the original inventor of the computer-aided engineering tools used for the JSF program: France's Dassault, which developed the CATIA design software used by Lockheed Martin and its partners, and by Boeing, for its commercial airplanes and applied it from the late 1980s in the definition of the carrier-based and land-based versions of the Rafale.

The mid-body section is put together around the propulsion system. The JSF is the largest single-engine fighter ever built, with a thrust requirement driven by vertical landing, and the engines are expected to produce more than 40,000 pounds of thrust with afterburner, significantly more than both the engines on an F-4 Phantom, which was regarded in its day as almost obscenely large for a fighter. The F-22's F119 engine, from which the Pratt & Whitney F135 is derived, produces more than 35,000 pounds of thrust but has a smaller bypass ratio, which makes it smaller in diameter because it handles less air. One program official has been quoted as saying that the JSF engines are almost 4 feet in diameter and that they weigh 6,000 pounds.

The engine is located relatively far forward because the vectoring nozzle cannot be placed at the extreme tail; it provides more than half the vertical thrust and the airplane could not be balanced otherwise. The inlet trunk forks sharply ahead of the engine and between the forks, behind the cockpit is another large bay for the STOVL version's lift fan.

Clearly visible are the large doors under the three-bearing swivel nozzle, the largest moving panels on the airplane. The doors in the STOVL system must be highly reliable, while being exposed to high-velocity airflow, noise, and vibration. They must close precisely after a STO to maintain the airplane's stealth characteristics.
Lockheed Martin

In a shaft-driven lift-fan system, the fan needs to be as large as possible. A principle of aircraft propulsion is that the slower the speed of the vehicle, the slower the speed of the air for best efficiency. Jets are not good for 200-mile-per-hour light airplanes, and the most efficient way to lift an aircraft vertically is with a rotor. The bigger, that is, more rotor-like, the lift-fan that the designers could squeeze into the JSF fuselage, the more thrust it would produce. The result is that the JSF forward fuselage—in all three versions—is designed around a vertical well, 50 inches in diameter, open at the top and bottom. In the CV and CTOL versions this space is used as a fuel tank.

The lift fan has two counter-rotating stages, one above and one below the input gear from the shaft. The thrust of the lift fan and the energy that it extracts from the main engine is controlled by inlet guide vanes which restrict the flow of air through the fan. To start the fan, the inlet guide vanes are closed and the clutch is engaged, taking three to seven seconds for the fan to reach the same speed as the engine. The clutch is then locked and the inlet vanes open as the engine is throttled up. At full power, the fan is extracting 28,000 shaft horsepower from the engine. By mid-2004, 1,500 clutch engagements had been performed during tests.

A straightforward design with a responsive and powerful engine, the X-35A encountered no difficulty in maintaining station behind the KC-135E tanker. Lockheed Martin

Like the F-117 and F-22, the F-35 has flattened body sides that are canted at the same angle as the vertical tails to reduce side-on radar cross-section. Lockheed Martin

The JSF is slender, clean, and powerful enough to exceed Mach 1.5. However, limiting the maximum Mach number reduces temperatures in the engine and simplifies the inlet design—and, as a bomber, JSF will largely operate at subsonic speeds. Lockheed Martin

The JSF will be delivered with a choice of engines, like the F-16 today. The engine is the only part of the JSF where the Pentagon has invested money in promoting competition within the program. A late-1990s Rand Corporation study of the value of competition in JSF production concluded that there was no economic justification for splitting the prime contract, but studiously avoided any mention of the engine, merely stating that the decision to compete the engine program had already been taken. A high-level review commissioned in late 1997 concluded that the alternate engine program (AEP) had "significant benefits" in terms of maintaining an industrial base and keeping contractors responsive, but that it would not reduce risk in SDD unless the GE-Rolls-Royce team was funded to match the schedule of the primary engine, which has not been done. If the leading engine, Pratt & Whitney's F135, falls behind schedule, so will the entire program. Benefits in terms of production costs would be marginal.

However, the AEP has been maintained for a number of reasons. The JSF was designed around an engine derived from the F-22's F119, and time constraints compelled the program to specify an F119-based engine for the concept demonstration phase. GE lobbied heavily to be given an opportunity to compete. Also, the Pentagon was concerned about the dangers of relying on a single engine core for the entire USAF fighter force, F/A-22s and F-35s, because there have been instances where serious engine problems have surfaced long after tests have been completed. Even the most intensive tests can only approximate the real environment of tactical flying, and modern jet engines can be sensitive to physically minute amounts of wear.

Both JSF engines are derived from the Pratt & Whitney F119 and GE YF120, developed for the advanced tactical fighter competition. They are both fixed-cycle turbofan engines with a higher bypass ratio about 0.5:1 more than the F119. The difference is that the JSF is not required to cruise at supersonic speed, so it does not need the F119's near-pure-jet cycle. Both engines feature high stage loadings; the Pratt & Whitney F135 has a six-stage high-pressure compressor, versus 10 horsepower stages on the F100 and single-stage high-pressure and low-pressure turbines. The two shafts rotate in opposite directions, eliminating a stator stage between the turbines.

Development of the Pratt & Whitney F135 engine started at the same time as the aircraft, and the first engine was tested at the end of 2003. Seven engines were under test by mid-2004 and had accumulated 500 test hours. At the same time, GE and Rolls-Royce were funded to start "pre-SDD" for the alternative F136 engine. SDD proper for the F136 will start in mid-2005. The F136 will make its first test runs in early 2007 and will be available from the fifth LRIP block onward.

A unique feature is that the two engines will be freely interchangeable, this is not the case on the F-16, and the differences between them will be transparent to the aircraft systems and the pilot. From a practical standpoint, GE- and P&W-powered aircraft will probably be segregated in different units, but they could be mixed in an emergency.

The main differences among the three F-35 versions concern their take-off and landing modes. The STOVL version has the lift fan installed in the forward bay, with the clutch attached to the fan case and linked to the shaft. It also has an auxiliary air inlet above the fuselage to keep the engine running at low-to-zero forward speeds. Large doors above and below the fan, and below the three-bearing swivel nozzle, open for jet-borne flight.

The STOVL hardware made the F-35B the heaviest of the three versions even before the weight growth that

The F-35A/B's clipped, moderately swept wing recalls its ancestor, the Lockheed Starfighter. The stabilizers are large, relative to the wing, and will require powerful actuators— some of which may account for the growth in the JSF's weight. Lockheed Martin

RIGHT: The production JSF will be rather sleeker than the prototypes, and the F-35A and F-35C will have more of an all-round-vision canopy. The USAF and navy versions will feature a stealth-compatible exhaust nozzle with a serrated edge. Lockheed Martin

emerged in 2003-2004. Its design operating weight was 3,300 pounds more than the CTOL version, and the latter carries a gun. Taking the weight growth into account, the STOVL system probably adds well over 4,000 pounds to the airplane's empty weight. The F-35B also has 5,000 pounds less internal fuel than either of the other two versions.

With a 620-square-foot wing, 35 percent larger than that of the F-35A and F-35B and actually bigger than an F-15's wing and a stronger structure to withstand carrier landings, the CV F-35C still has a design empty weight fractionally less than that of the STOVL airplane. It has the largest internal fuel capacity of the three versions, some 1,100 pounds more than the F-35A, which gives it the greatest range—a hi-lo-hi combat radius of 800 nautical miles with internal fuel and weapons. The F-35C has more fuel than the USAF version because it does not have an internal gun, and because it has a retractable refueling probe in the nose (so does the F-35B) rather than a boom receptacle in the upper fuselage. However, the F-35C is likely to be slower in acceleration then the F-35A, particularly at transonic speeds, because of its larger wing.

Despite its origins in a program called the Common Affordable lightweight fighter, the JSF is no lightweight. Even without weight growth, the CV and STOVL versions have operating empty weights comparable to an F-15E Strike Eagle and (as noted above) more power than an F-4. The CV version has a clean take-off weight—without external stores—of more than 55,000 pounds, and up to 13,000 pounds of external weapons, for a maximum take-off weight of 68,000 pounds. The JSF has seven external stores stations: the inner wing stations are designed to carry 5,000 pounds, for instance, a 600 gallon fuel tank, and the mid-wing stations carry 2,500 pounds, typically two 1,000-pound guided bombs on a dual rack.

With this substantial weight, even the JSF's enormous engine is not going to make it a spectacular performer in the air. Full afterburner will get the aircraft motivated, certainly, but at a huge price in fuel consumption. The engines deliver 26,000 to 27,000 pounds of thrust without afterburner, which will be adequate for acceleration in clean condition, but is not a lot compared with the maximum gross weight; the F-16 Block 60 has more than 20,000 pounds of military power but is one-third lighter. The CV and STOVL versions have a wing area slightly greater than that of the F/A-18C/D, but are substantially heavier. The performance numbers are clear: JSF is, essentially, a bomber.

Part of the airplane's size can be accounted for by stealth, which has affected the design in many ways. The JSF's stealth capability is essential to the Pentagon's

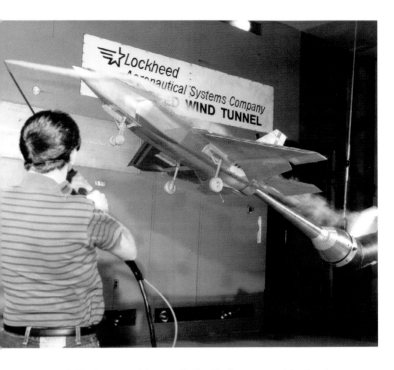

Early stealth advocates believed that their aircraft would be invisible, and virtually invulnerable to air defenses regardless of tactics. This belief was exploded by "Red Team" operational analysis in the late 1970s, leading to the development of computer-based mission planning systems to support the F-117 and B-2. These systems developed complex routes which would minimize the attackers' exposure to known radars.

The logical next step, attempted at great cost and with modest success in the B-2 program, was to provide the aircraft with a real-time system to detect, locate and identify emitters, and estimate their ability to detect the aircraft. Even so, the tactical concept behind the LO aircraft was similar to that of a submarine: the stealth aircraft would operate alone, with a bare minimum of emissions and no non-stealthy support aircraft in the area.

Most operational stealth missions, however, have been supported by other assets. It has been stated that all USAF missions during Allied Force,

The larger wing of the Navy airplane undergoes low-speed wind-tunnel testing. Another distinguishing feature is the dual-wheel nose landing gear with an aft link that transmits catapult loads into the fuselage.

The F-35 will have separate multi-spar wings bolted to a carry-through structure that comprises several forged and machined bulkheads spanning the mid-fuselage structure. The inlets curve sharply around the lift-fan bay, which is used as a fuel tank on the F-35A and F-35C. Lockheed Martin

ability to convert to an all-stealth force—an objective in 1985, which was expected to be achieved in 2000. Had plans been in place at that time been realized, the United States would have had 800 stealth aircraft in service by 2002, including 130-plus B-2 bombers and two wings of fully operational F-22s, with two more working up. Half the navy's carrier air wings would include attack squadrons with long-range, heavy-payload A-12s. More than 150 A-12s and F-22s would be rolling off production lines.

These goals were not achieved partly because operational LO aircraft proved harder and more expensive to develop and produce than expected, but mainly because the technology matured just as the Soviet Union collapsed, heralding a decade in which major military aircraft procurement ground to a halt and budgets were reduced. JSF was conceived as a lower-cost substitute for the A-12 and for many of the F-22s.

The JSF reflects changes in stealth technology and the way in which it is used. The most important change, part of a trend reaching back to the earliest days of stealth, is that LO is one part of the survivability equation and not a panacea.

including F-117 and B-2 sorties, were supported by EA-6B Prowler escort jammers, while F-117 missions in Desert Storm benefited from both jamming and the distraction caused by simultaneous attacks by other weapons, including Tomahawk cruise missiles. The USAF, which retired its dedicated defense-suppression aircraft (F-4G Wild Weasels) and escort jammers (EF-111A Ravens) in the 1990s, now relies on F-16s and navy EA-6Bs to fill these roles. Officially, the USAF considers that the B-2 is survivable "on the assumption that appropriate mission planning, *force packaging*, and tactics are employed."

A Lockheed engineer claimed in 1991 that stealth would cause active jamming "to go the way of the buggy-whip industry," but this has not happened. Stealth and active jamming from offboard platforms work together, because an escort jammer can be effective over a much wider area if the real echo that must be masked is smaller. For the foreseeable future, stealth aircraft will operate as part of mixed forces

The shootdown of an F-117 over Serbia in April 1999 sent ripples through the LO community. The USAF has not

revealed its final conclusions as to the cause of the shootdown, but a combination of factors was probably to blame. Support assets were not all in the right place at the right time. The SA-3 site that hit the aircraft had not been properly located. F-117s had flown repeated missions to the same targets over the same tracks, and the aircraft involved had just released a weapon, potentially creating a momentarily strong radar return.

The F-117 shoot-down confirmed that LO aircraft become much more vulnerable when surprise is lost, even if the adversary uses rudimentary systems to cue defensive systems in the attacker's likely flight-path. One consequence is that LO aircraft still cannot be used in daylight because of the risk that a visual observation from the ground or the air will lead to an interception. According to Air Combat Command Chief Gen. John Jumper, "the greatest problem we have today with the F-117 and the B-2 . . . is that they can't protect themselves from air-to-air and visually directed air-to-surface threats."

The first stealth aircraft were designed to carry only offensive weapons, but this is changing. A pair of internally

The three-bearing nozzle is a straight pipe with three angled segments that can rotate relative to one another. By rotating the segments in opposite directions, the nozzle can be made to rotate through 100 degrees and move to left and right. Rolls-Royce

The X-35's STOVL propulsion system was tested at full scale at West Palm Beach before the aircraft flew. In STOVL mode, a vast number of functions—from guide vane settings in the fan to fuel flow and exhaust nozzle positions—are controlled automatically to make the JSF respond to the controls, requiring a huge amount of flight-critical software. Pratt & Whitney

Large-diameter ring gears are used to rotate the segments of the three-bearing nozzle on the STOVL F-35. Rolls-Royce

The F-35's inlet ducts are curved to fit around the lift fan bay and to conceal the face of the engine from radar. The shape ensures that any radar signals reflected from the compressor will bounce off the duct walls several times before they escape, and are attenuated each time by the radar-absorbent coatings inside the duct. Lockheed Martin

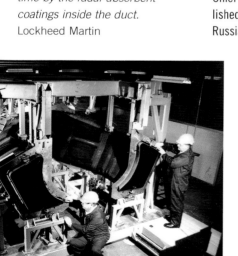

carried AIM-120 AMRAAMs has been a basic element of the JSF requirement from the start of the program, and will allow JSF to counter hostile fighters beyond visual range. A JSF will not necessarily use its own radar to guide AMRAAM; electronic signals from the target, infra-red search and track information or a radar track from another JSF, out of range of the target, will suffice.

The threats and targets against which stealth aircraft are intended to operate have also changed. Former USAF Chief of Staff General Ron Fogleman, in an interview published in early 2001, commented that clandestine tests of Russian surface-to-air missiles were a surprise to the USAF.

"One of the side benefits of the end of the cold war was our gaining access to foreign weapons," said Fogleman. "We discovered that the SA-10s, -11s, and -12s are much better than we thought." In the 1996 Taiwan Straits crisis, says Fogleman, "we sent two carriers in and watched the Chinese move their SA-10s up." With the even more powerful long-range S-400 (SA-20) system under development and offered for export, the USAF's anxiety about its non-stealthy aircraft is reaching a higher pitch.

Despite the fall of the Soviet Union and the absence, anywhere in the world, of a highly integrated air defense system (IADS) of the kind that had been installed in Central Europe, SAMs still

present a threat. Increasingly, stealth is seen as a way of permitting unrestricted air operations over hostile territory at any time. One very important reason for the Bush administration's endorsement of the JSF program was that, without an LO aircraft, the navy's carrier air wings would have been increasingly incapable of operating in the face of an intensifying SAM threat.

The JSF's stealth technology is based on that of the Lockheed Martin F-22 Raptor, which started its inflight RCS tests in January 2001. Lockheed Martin claims that the fighter will represent a considerable advance in "affordable stealth," due to changes in design philosophy, development processes, and LO materials.

The close family resemblance between the F-22 and JSF is no coincidence, but is dictated by the basic principles of stealth. In fact, if you look at the F-22 in front view and turn the picture upside-down, you can clearly see the lines of the F-117, albeit with the addition of some gently curved surfaces and the rounding-off of the sharp lines between the facets.

In fact, Lockheed engineers believed, even before the F-117 was built, that they could back away from the uncompromisingly faceted shape of the Have Blue demonstrator. What they could not do was show that the signatures of such a smoothed-out shape could be modeled and predicted accurately, from computer to RCS range and from RCS range to a flying prototype, and the customer was not ready to accept that amount of risk so that F-117 emerged with no curvature or rounding. However, some of the changes in shape were incorporated on Lockheed's next stealth design, the unsuccessful competitor to the B-2, and in the advanced tactical fighter designs which led to the F-22.

Lockheed stealth pioneer Denys Overholser has defined the four most important elements of stealth as "shape, shape, shape, and materials." The JSF's shape may look conventional and is familiar, given that its twin-engine cousin, the F-22, flew in prototype form a decade and a half ago, but in fact, its configuration, external lines, and internal arrangement are largely defined by stealth concerns.

In terms of weight, performance, and overall balance of the design, the most important stealth-driven feature of

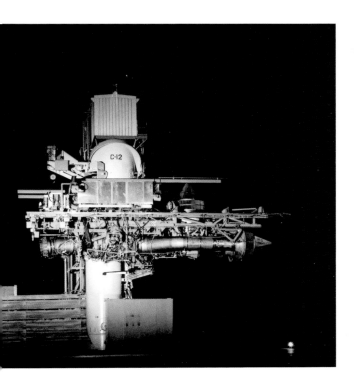

the JSF's configuration is that it carries a 5,000-pound internal weapon load; by comparison, a World War II B-17 typically carried 6,000 pounds of bombs and carried internal fuel amounting to almost 40 percent of its take-off weight. Apart from some heavy U.S. interceptors of the 1950s, fighters have historically carried weapons on external pylons, for good reason. Although bombs, missiles, and stores racks generate extra drag on the ingress leg of a mission, they still have less impact on the fighter's size and range than an internal weapons bay designed to carry a wide variety of bombs and missiles. The entire airplane has to be scaled up to make room for the weapon bay, and that extra weight and volume must be carried at all times, inbound and outbound.

As for fuel, very few fighters fly routinely without external fuel tanks. Carrying drop tanks is not very efficient; the tanks themselves cause extra drag, but they can be dumped before supersonic combat and allow the fighter to be smaller and lighter for a given radius of action. They also make it possible to trade fuel for weapons, making the fighter more versatile.

There is another reason why the need to carry internal weapons and fuel tends to make a stealthy fighter bigger. Successful fighter airplanes have a very long lifetime; the F-16 is still going strong after three decades in production. Like most of us, they gain weight. The new F-16E/F Desert Falcon for the United Arab Emirates has a maximum take-off weight that is 50 percent higher than that of the original F-16A/B. The weight increase allows the airplane to carry more equipment—internal electronic jamming systems and external targeting pods, for example—and heavier weapons.

Weight growth has been offset by increased thrust; the Desert Falcon's General Electric F110-GE-132 engine provides 90 percent as much thrust in military power as the original A/B's F100 put out in full burner. But more thrust would be of little use without more fuel, the engine is much more powerful but not much more efficient so the E/F carries

Top view of a lift fan shows its large size, and the inlet guide vanes which regulate the fan's power. The vanes are closed to their lowest power setting to start the fan, reducing the load on the clutch and engine, and are opened once the fan is up to speed and the clutch is locked. Rolls-Royce

The lift fan has two stages, spun in opposite directions by a single beveled input gear. Each stage is a "blisk:" during manufacture, the wide-chord, swept fan blades are bonded to the disk, rather than being attached to it with a slotted fitting and bolts. Rolls-Royce

600-gallon underwing tanks, rather than the 370-gallon tanks carried by older F-16s, and a pair of conformal tanks above the fuselage that carry another 450 gallons of fuel. The two-seat F-16F has a boxy dorsal spine, accommodating equipment that is displaced by the rear

seat, and that would elbow out internal fuel if it were located anywhere else.

This can't be done with a stealth aircraft. The outer mold line cannot be easily changed without sacrificing the fighter's stealth qualities. Weight, weapon load, and thrust growth are limited by the fact that there is no stealthy way to add extra fuel: the airplane is stuck with the fuel capacity that it's given in the preliminary design stage. This is one reason why the F-35 is not a small airplane.

Adding weapon bays and more internal fuel is a particularly serious problem for a supersonic, agile fighter. A jet engine at full afterburner consumes fuel at an awesome rate, and the drag caused when the airplane accelerates through Mach 1 is strongly influenced by its cross-sectional area and the airplane's length in relation to its girth. Adding volume at the middle of the airplane, which is where the weapon bay has to be because otherwise releasing weapons will make the airplane nose- or tail-heavy, is bad, as drag increases. If the fighter is also intended to pull 9 g in combat, too, the last thing that the designer wants to do

is cut big holes in the skin, because the metal or carbon-fiber skin and the structure beneath it carry the flight loads.

In fact, the JSF has already suffered from weight growth that is due in part to its internal layout. Under the skin, the fighter's configuration is unusual and not quite like that of the F-22. The center section is largely occupied by three empty spaces: the weapon bays, the inlet duct and engine tunnel, and the cavity for the lift fan. The JSF is smaller than the F-22, but the weapon bays are deeper; the fattest weapon that will fit in the F-22 is the 1,000-pound GBU-32 bomb, while the JSF will fit a 2,000-pound GBU-31.

The F-22's twin engines and split weapon bay allow for a central full-depth keel from top to bottom of the center section, which carries the bending loads encountered in a 9 g turn. Moreover, this is a logical location for fuel lines, hydraulic lines, and electrical connections. There is no place for such a structure on the JSF, because the engine tunnel is in the way. The result is that all the lines, hoses, and wires have to be routed around the outside of the tunnel; a process that did not prove easy.

Another key, stealth-driven feature is the inlet design. Concealing the front of the engine from radar is crucial: not only is the compressor face, with its rotating blades, a major RCS contributor, but a modern, smart radar can

Rolls-Royce also makes the multi-stage clutch that connects the output shaft from the engine to the input gear on the fan. The multi-disk clutch has some features in common with the stacked brakes used on large commercial airplanes, storing friction energy as heat and releasing it once the clutch plates are locked. Rolls-Royce

The X-35 runs its engine at full power. The F135 engine on the production airplane has a bypass ratio of around 0.5:1 and is the most powerful engine on any fighter aircraft. Lockheed Martin

The low observable axisymmetric nozzle (LOAN) uses an ejector to mix the air that cools the outside of the engine with the hot exhaust stream, resulting in a lower infra-red signature than a conventional nozzle, and uses scalloped edges and radar-absorbent materials to reduce its radar signature. It is lighter and less costly than the two-dimensional nozzle on the F/A-22. Lockheed Martin

actually use that signal to identify its target because the spinning blades produce a characteristic beat in the echo determined by engine RPM and the number of blades, and a technique called jet engine modulation (JEM) can be used to identify an aircraft.

The grill-covered inlets on the F-117 were unacceptable for the F-22 and JSF, for the simple reason that, as the airplane approaches Mach 1, shock waves form on the grills and the inlet chokes. The alternative approach is a more conventional inlet, but with a curved "serpentine" duct which blocks the line of sight to the engine's compressor face. This would not conceal the engine face from radar on its own: the radar signal will bounce off the duct wall to reach the engine and will eventually bounce out. However, the duct walls are treated with radar absorbent material (RAM), which gradually attenuates the energy with each successive bounce until the escaping signal is too small to be detected.

The F-22 uses a "scarfed and swept" raked-back inlet, meaning the lips are angled in three dimensions, but it

was relatively heavy and complicated because of the need to scoop away the "boundary layer" of turbulent air along the fuselage side. There is a slot between the inlet and the body, with a bypass system that captures the turbulent air in the slot and dumps it overboard.

The JSF uses a unique and much simpler inlet. Instead of a slot, it features a shallow, smooth bump on the body side, positioned between upper and lower inlet lips that slant forward, away from the body. The bump creates a pressure rise, and the result is that the boundary layer is gently diverted to either side, like a stream flowing around a smooth rock. The inlet is simple and stealthy, and provides adequate performance at supersonic speed; unlike the F-22, the JSF is not intended to cruise at Mach 1.7 and it performs most of its mission at subsonic speed, so some sacrifice in efficiency is acceptable. However, the entire inlet is longer and more complex than a non-stealthy inlet and takes up more volume.

Externally, the JSF's stealth features are based on the same principles as Have Blue. The foundation of this technique is a very simple fact: a flat surface has both the largest and smallest RCS of any object. Illuminated at right angles, it is huge. But as it is tilted or canted away from the beam in one dimension, its RCS decreases sharply; reflectivity is reduced by a factor of 1,000 at a cant angle of 30 degrees. If the same surface is rotated away from the beam on a diagonal axis, that is to say it is both canted and swept back; the RCS reduction is much greater, so that the same reduction can be realized at an 8 degrees angle.

The trick to Have Blue was that Lockheed's engineers found a way to design an airplane which was made entirely out of flat surfaces, canted and rotated away from the arrival angle of any radar beam. What made this possible was that some radars were more dangerous than others: the radars in front of and behind the aircraft. The side-on view is tactically less important; as an aircraft flies past a radar that is located on one side of its flight-path, the radar is directly on the airplane's beam for only a moment. The result is that most stealth aircraft have a "bow-tie" RCS picture: if you chart the RCS or detection range from above the aircraft, it blooms on both sides and is narrow at the nose and tail, where it matters most.

F135 engine under assembly at Pratt & Whitney. The isogrid pattern on the casing is produced by chemical etching before the case is rolled into its final shape. Like its cousin, the F119, the F135 will be built so that it can be maintained with a small set of tools, and without time-consuming features such as safety-wired fasteners.
Pratt & Whitney

If the airplane was to be made out of flat surfaces it would also have edges where they met. Again, Have Blue was designed so that those edges were swept forwards or backwards, away from the radar beam. That effect is less apparent on the JSF, where some of those edges are rounded; but the predominant feature of the body shape is still its flat, canted sides.

The principle of dealing with wing and tail edges on the JSF is also basically the same used on Have Blue or even on the original "Hopeless Diamond" study: sweep them, backwards or forwards, so that they are not at right angles to the most threatening radars and make the shape out of a minimum number of long edges.

The longer the edge, the better it focuses the radar return. This may seem to be a bad thing, but consider the geometry of an aircraft with long edges passing through an area illuminated by a radar that is not directly on its flight-path. At one point only, the radar beam will be at right angles to the long leading edge, and the radar can see its echo, but the phenomenon is transient. The geometry will be less than optimal at the radar sweep before it, and less than optimal after it.

An important extension of this discipline, very apparent on JSF, is the way that edges are aligned. For example, the trailing edges of the wing are aligned with the trailing edges of the horizontal stabilizer and with the upper and lower inlet lips on the opposite side of the airplane. The wing and tail leading edges are aligned with each other. The idea is that it is better to add energy to the "spikes" in the radar signature at right angles to each of the sharp edges than to add more spikes, even small ones, which increase the probability of detection.

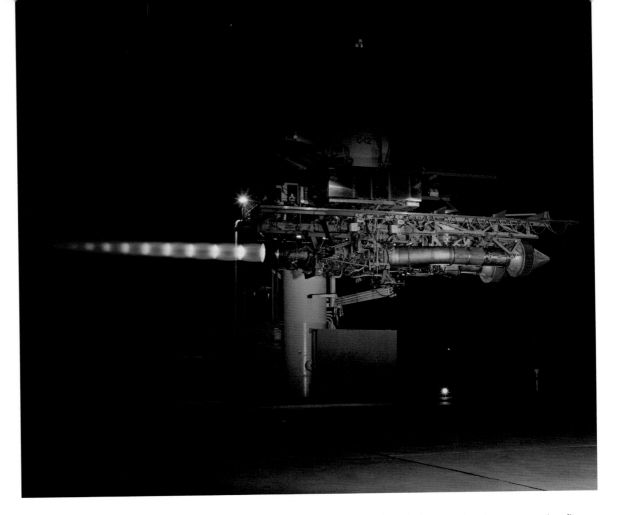

From the F-117 onward, this edge alignment was extended to all the apertures on the airplane. One of the many complexities of military airplane design is that the aircraft is packed with complex systems: hydraulics, electronics, fuel lines, sensors, and so on, which have to be accessible for maintenance and repair. The F-15 has 570 square feet of hinged or removable access panels, roughly equivalent to the area of the fighter's wing.

For a stealth aircraft, apertures are awkward. A door or panel that fits perfectly in aerodynamic terms can create an electromagnetic discontinuity and cause an unacceptable RCS spike. On Have Blue, access panels were caulked or taped before every flight; on later airplanes, including the JSF, panels that must be accessible, as well as landing gear, weapon bay doors, and the cockpit opening, are designed so that their edges follow the primary alignments. Where this would be structurally difficult, the edges are serrated so that the aperture is basically square.

Even the best design cannot make an access door fit precisely or eliminate a reflection from an edge, which is where materials come in. One lesson from crude, early attempts at stealth was that there is no radar absorbent material (RAM) that is magic enough to hide a badly shaped airplane. Conversely, there is no shaping technique yet devised that can yield a practical stealth airplane without RAM.

The F-117 was almost entirely covered with RAM, a polymer material resembling linoleum floor covering in density, which contributed nothing to the airframe's strength but added a ton to its weight. On the JSF, RAM and radar absorbent structure (RAS) are used more selectively. Most of the surface will be covered with a conductive metallic coating which prevents radar energy from penetrating the composite skin.

Lockheed Martin has developed paint-type RAM which is applied around the edges of doors and control surfaces, and radar absorbent structure (RAS) on the body, wing,

capacity to provide 1,000 typical homes. Robots are essential because humans cannot work in confined areas, such as the inlet duct, and because long-reach robots do not have to walk on the airplane's surface. CASPER, the computer aided spray paint expelling robot, has been developed to paint the F-22's inlet ducts.

The JSF is expected to use similar techniques, but with refinements to reduce cost. For example, the robotic spray system will be based on technology used in the Have Glass II program, under which RAM coatings have been applied to more than 1,700 F-16s.

Basically, these surface coatings comprise ferromagnetic particles; the best for most applications, embedded in a high-dielectric-constant polymer base. The dielectric material slows the wave down, and the ferromagnetic particles absorb the energy. However, Lockheed Martin also designed its coatings so that the small reflection from the front face of the absorber is cancelled by a residual reflection from the structure beneath it. The first step is to make the total pathway of energy within the RAM equal to half a wavelength so that the residual reflection is exactly out-of-phase with the front-face reflection.

The RAM can be much thinner than the nominal wavelength of the radar and still achieve cancellation because the wavelength inside the material is much shorter than it is in free space. Also, refraction within the RAM keeps the internal path length close to constant over a wide range of incidence angles.

Finally, the absorption of the RAM is tailored so that the energy which travels through the RAM, bounces off the substructure and escapes exactly equal in magnitude to the front-face reflection. Stealth pioneer Alan Brown's comment that RAM design is "much more tricky than you would think at first sight" is a classic understatement.

Solid RAM coatings cover a frequency range of about 20:1. This is enough to address air-to-air and surface-to-air missile radars (from the L-band up to the Ku-band) but more elaborate schemes are used to cover the full radar spectrum, including low-frequency VHF radars such as the Russian-made P-14 (codenamed Tall King) and its Chinese equivalents.

and tail edges. As on the F-22, paints and coatings will be applied by robots under carefully controlled conditions. Temperature, humidity, and airflow have to be maintained within tight parameters and adjusted constantly through the coating cycle, and the painting chambers themselves are supported by a massive infrastructure of power lines and ducts. The F-22 painting chamber has enough cooling

These radars affect the target in different ways. Brown compares a typical wide-band radar absorbent structure (RAS), used on the edges of a stealth aircraft, to "a stereo system with a tweeter and a woofer." The "tweeter" is a high-frequency ferromagnetic absorber like the coating described above, applied over a resistive layer that reflects higher frequencies but allows low-frequency signals to pass through. Beneath this resistive layer is the low-frequency "woofer:" a glass-fiber honeycomb core, treated from front to back with a steadily increasing amount of resistive material. Brown calls it "an electromagnetic shock absorber. It's very soft in front, but we still absorb pretty much all the energy inside, because we don't want the energy to hit the vertical front face of the structure."

The fighter's infra-red (IR) signature will not be neglected. The entire airframe will be painted with a camouflage topcoat which suppresses IR. The infra-red search and track (IRST) system under development for the EuroFighter Typhoon has been credited with a range of more than 60 miles against conventional targets such as Tornados and

MiG-29s. Detection ranges for the JSF will presumably be much shorter.

Lockheed Martin engineers tried to take advantage of hard-earned lessons in the development of the LO systems materials, coatings, and seals in the design of the JSF. Many of these lessons were also applied to the F-22. For example, the F-22 LO development program exclusively used full-scale models, following problems in earlier programs where data from subscale models proved unreliable as a predictor of full-scale results. The radar-cross-section (RCS) test program started with partial models, including an inlet, a radome, and a dual-engine afterbody model. This culminated in tests of a high-fidelity full-scale model, which started in 1999. The model included a radar, all doors and even the first two stages of the engines, and all control surfaces could be actuated by remote control.

On the JSF program, a similarly detailed model—the signature measurement aircraft (SigMA)—was built and tested much earlier, during the CDA stage. Even the first JSF model was highly detailed and included control surfaces and doors. Again, the objective is to reduce the risk of surprises during testing.

Maintainability has also been a key issue. On the first stealth aircraft, the need to reduce RCS was emphasized above all else. The number of openings and apertures was

limited in many ways. For example, systems were installed so that they could be reached through the landing gear or weapons bay doors and materials were selected according to their stealth properties and how well they worked in a specific location on the airframe. On the B-2, the result was that the bomber used dozens of different materials, each of which had its own supply chain and required its own maintenance and handling training. Some of those materials, it was known from the outset, could only be removed and restored slowly, laboriously, and under carefully controlled conditions. For example, some of the caulks used to seal gaps had to be applied in an air-conditioned hangar, and only a few feet could be applied before the material was left to cure.

One key change on the F-22 is that the fighter uses about one-third as many different types of LO material as earlier stealth aircraft. The remaining materials have been selected and developed for durability and maintainability as well as their LO performance.

To avoid the need to repair LO seals and coatings in the field, the F-22 has almost 300 specially designed access points. These include quick-access panels featuring positive locks, seals, and gaskets. Many service points are located inside the weapon bays, landing gear doors and other openings. The goal is to ensure that 95 percent of all maintenance actions in a 30-day deployment can be performed without removing material.

The same standards are being applied to the F-35, in a more demanding environment, including austere bases and aircraft carriers. Two-thirds of all maintenance actions can be performed through actuated doors. Most of the remaining third use hinged, latched, and fastened doors, rather than removable panels. Components such as sample quick-access doors, radome boots, in-flight opening doors (landing gears and weapon bays), and sealants were tested in flight on F-16s and the X-35s as well as on the SigMA.

Other new goals for the F-35 include a "life of aircraft" skin coating, which is expected to last 8,000 hours under tactical conditions without being repaired or replaced, except in the case of impact damage; and a door-edge design that can tolerate impact damage without losing its stealth properties.

Better materials and designs are part of the solution to stealth maintenance problems. However, it is also vital to know whether LO material has been damaged, whether a detectable flaw is actually going to cause the airplane to be more visible on radar, or whether a repair has fixed the problem. This requires the ability to diagnose problems and confirm that repairs have worked.

In early stealth aircraft, the only ways to ensure that the aircraft was performing to specification were either to maintain it perfectly, removing and replacing LO material at the slightest sign of damage, or to measure the airplane's entire signature, using a ground-based radar mounted on tracks

Full-size radar cross-section "pole model" on the pylon at Lockheed Martin's Helendale, California, test facility. The airplane is mounted upside down so that the test radars—at the end of a carefully graded strip a mile away—can get a clear unobstructed image of its underside, the most likely viewing angle for a ground-based radar. Lockheed Martin

Photo of an unpainted F-22 shows some of the different layers of radar-absorbent coating and materials. Wing and tail edges and inlet lips all comprise a gray radar-absorbent structure (RAS). Access doors are treated with RAM, and a green yellow primer covers much of the structure—it will later be covered by an IR-absorbing topcoat. *Lockheed Martin*

to image the airplane from all angles. The USAF and Boeing have been working for some years to develop an improved, automated diagnostic radar called the common LO verification system (CLOVerS), but even with the latest equipment, such tests are time-consuming and the equipment itself represents an added burden when a unit is deployed away from its main base. Moreover, such a system could be very inconvenient to use on an aircraft carrier.

The goal for JSF is to make visual inspection the cornerstone of LO maintenance. Ground crews will inspect the aircraft and enter any damage data on a portable computer. The damage will automatically be compared to a fleet-wide database to determine if a repair is necessary. As the database on the "effects of defects" and "effects of repairs" expands, only the most major repairs will need to be verified using portable or hand-held tools which measure material thickness, reflectivity, and resistivity. Only rarely will the entire aircraft need to be checked. While today's stealth aircraft are routinely checked by airborne RCS measurement systems, that approach is not affordable for thousands of JSFs.

More testing is scheduled to make sure that these goals are being met. For the first time in any LO program, a real airframe will be used exclusively for tests on an RCS

range, alongside a range of fixtures to test detailed components. Materials and doors will continue to be tested on USAF F-16s, a carrier-based F/A-18, and a Marine Corps AV-8B Harrier (the last test will expose materials to the hot, noisy environment of a jet-lift aircraft).

Internally, JSF will pioneer another major change in technology, which stems indirectly from work under the strategic defense initiative (SDI) or "Star Wars" program in the 1980s. Looking at the need to put powerful electrical systems on spacecraft, SDI researchers developed new ways of converting and controlling electrical power in lightweight, solid-state packages. This technology now makes it practical to use electrical power to replace the high-pressure hydraulic systems which move the airplane's flight controls, landing gear, and other components. Electrical wiring requires less maintenance than hydraulic lines and is less vulnerable to combat damage.

The USAF was working on this technology before JSF started, and had concluded that the logical extension was to develop an integrated system that would replace all the mechanical accessories which are normally connected to the fighter's engine. This effort was absorbed by JSF, and was known as JSF Integrated Subsystems Technology (J/IST).

J/IST demonstration contracts were shared between the two teams, and the results were available to both sides. Lockheed Martin led the inflight demonstration of electric technology, and modified the hard-worked advanced fighter technology integration (AFTI) F-16 prototype as the first fighter to fly with all its primary flight controls both signaled and powered by electricity, and with no mechanical backup.

Developed and tested by Boeing, the other element of J/IST replaced a number of complex systems in today's fighters. A modern fighter engine has a "tower shaft" which links the high-pressure spool of the engine to an airframe-mounted accessory drive (AMAD). The AMAD is a compact package of gears, clutches, and constant-speed drives that, in turn, drive the hydraulic pumps, electrical generators, and the environmental control system (ECS)

compressor. A gas-turbine auxiliary power unit (APU) or an emergency power unit may also be connected to the AMAD, to start the engine and to power essential systems when the engine is not running.

On the production F-35, the core of the new secondary power system—known as the power and thermal management system—is a "turbo-machine" supplied by Honeywell. This comprises three components on a single shaft: a cooling turbine that circulates air through the primary ECS cooling loop; a 270-volt DC electric starter/generator, which is the aircraft's secondary electrical power source and starts the turbo-machine; and a power turbine, which is normally driven by engine bleed air and also incorporates a small combustor. The engine's tower shaft is connected to a second starter/generator, and there is no mechanical connection

X-35B on the hover pit. Six sets of doors—fan inlet and exhaust, auxiliary engine inlet, aft nozzle covers, and roll duct covers—open and close for each flight cycle. If they don't seal exactly, the airplane will not be stealthy in the air (and there is no direct way for the pilot to know that) and if they do not all open, the aircraft cannot land vertically. Lockheed Martin

A well-defined stream of hot air surges from the aft exhaust of the X-35B in an early hover test. The air around the rest of the airplane is cool and calm—but that is because it is above the hover pit, so hot air is passing through the cover grating and being ducted away from the airplane. Lockheed Martin

JSF will also take advantage of new technologies and disciplines in manufacturing. Military aircraft are among the most expensive weapons produced, and certainly the most expensive weapons that are routinely produced in triple-digit numbers. At the same time, their cost and capability have increased continuously since the first days of air warfare and production rates have decreased correspondingly. In 1967, McDonnell Douglas built 72 F-4s a month, an unimaginable rate today.

In 1986, Normal Augustine, president of Martin-Marietta, projected those trends and concluded that, by 2054, the entire U.S. defense budget would buy one aircraft. The U.S. Air Force and Navy would each use it for three-and-a-half days each week and the marines would be able to fly it for one day in each leap year.

Augustine's logic was recognized by some planners within the USAF and industry, resulting in an initiative called "factory of the future." The advanced tactical fighter, it was predicted at the time, would be built in highly automated factories, and labor-intensive tasks such as installing wiring and fluid lines would be taken away from humans and handled by sophisticated, multi-tasking robots.

X-35B prepares for a vertical landing, having slowed into a hover. Using the throttle to adjust for any wind speed so that the airplane is static over the ground, the pilot can now push forward on the stick to command a descent rate, which will be held automatically until the airplane touches down.
Lockheed Martin

At touchdown, long-stroke oleos absorb any remaining descent rate and ensure that the airplane does not bounce. The pilot can then pull the engine back to idle. A vertical landing is considered easier than a carrier landing and requires a smaller fuel reserve.
Lockheed Martin

between the engine and the turbo-machine. In effect, the turbo-machine is an electrical starter and generator, an auxiliary power unit, and an ECS turbine in a single unit.

To start the aircraft or provide power on the ground, the turbo-machine operates as a gas turbine APU using outside air. In flight, it is driven by engine bypass air and provides electrical power and cool air. In the event of an engine flame-out or stall, the turbo-machine is driven by compressed air stored in an onboard reservoir, maintaining essential power to the aircraft's controls until the pilot can get the JSF pointed downhill and perform an air-start.

The misunderstanding behind "the factory of the future" was that aircraft production rates are, and probably always will be, orders of magnitude less than the rates at which cars or other consumer goods are built. Honda builds one million vehicles per year in the United States alone. Investing massive sums in robotic factories to build a few hundred units, it became clear, was a fool's bet.

Instead, aircraft manufacturing is moving towards a doctrine known as "lean manufacturing." Based on an early-1990s study of Toyota and other leading manufacturers by the Massachusetts Institute of Technology, that was popularized in the book *The Machine That Changed the World*, lean is a discipline that focuses on seeking out and destroying all forms of waste in the production process. It does not eschew automation, but uses computer-controlled machines to do what they do best while recognizing that human beings are intelligent and flexible. Advanced technology plays a part but so do very simple measures, which are often initiated on the factory floor. Lean manufacturing is a journey, not an end, and stresses continuous improvement.

The X-35B lands vertically after the "hat-trick" flight—see the emblem on the tail—in which it made a short take-off, accelerated to supersonic speed, and made a vertical landing. The rival Boeing design could not do this, because it could not land vertically with its inlet jaw in place and could not go supersonic without it.
Lockheed Martin

Large, adjustable, mobile tools like this will be used for F-35 assembly. Rather than installing massive, steel, concrete-anchored tools to hold parts in position, F-35 assembly will rely on adjustable fixtures moved by electrical actuators and guided by lasers. Lockheed Martin

Lean manufacturing came into an industry where there was a great deal of room for such improvement. Production patterns and very often the systems used to buy parts and schedule work on the production line dated back to World War II. The industry's dirty secret was that these had never worked very well but nobody else did any better and the costs were passed on to the customer. The work was done, inspected and then, all too often, laboriously put right. "If you have to take an airplane and build it twice, it gets pretty damn expensive," one manager says.

Lean can use very simple techniques to bring about major improvements. As lean started to catch hold of the aerospace industry, and specialists started to look for waste on production lines, workers quickly pointed out that they spent a great deal of time hunting for necessary parts that, for one reason or another, were not to be found at their stations. Boeing's F/A-18 line used to have a state-of-the-art, centralized, automated system for storing and dispensing parts. It has now been removed and replaced by smaller parts bins, located no more than 12 paces away from the operator. Each bin has colored flags that the operator sets to indicate if they need to be refilled. For some operations, parts are supplied shrink-wrapped to a large sheet of cardboard, pre-printed with the shape and number of the parts needed. The assembler can tell instantly if there are any parts missing and what they are.

One overriding principle of lean production, as a Boeing manager puts it, is that "the mechanic assembly worker is a surgeon, and the airplane is the patient. The surgeon never leaves the patient." On older production lines, it was the mechanic's job to gather the drawings, parts, and tools for his shift from separate locations around the production floor. In lean production, everything needed for the job is delivered to the workplace as a complete kit. A specialist

organization makes sure that a kit is always ready when it is needed.

Similar techniques have been applied to Lockheed Martin's F-16 line, allowing the company to go from 180 aircraft a year in the early 1990s to a few tens of aircraft a year, while improving quality and reducing cost. Parts that used to be built in-house are now produced by subcontractors.

1980s robotic cells have been removed. Rather than trying to automate tasks, the production line has been changed to allow people to perform them more efficiently.

The JSF line will take advantage of some advances in technology. One of the most important is high-speed machining (HSM), originated in Europe in the 1980s and introduced by Boeing's Phantom Works to the U.S. aerospace industry. High-speed refers to the spindle speed of the carbide-tipped routers which are used to carve metal into complex shapes. The first generation of HSM technology raised spindle speeds from the low thousands of RPM to 10,000 RPM and more; today's machines run at 30,000 RPM.

HSM has many benefits. The faster spindles remove material faster and increase cutting speeds in linear feet per minute. More speed equals less force, and this makes it possible to machine components with thinner walls, which older and slower machines would have buckled and crushed. The result is that HSM can be used to make light-weight ribs and bulkheads that would previously have been made from complex built-up sheet-metal structures.

In final assembly, JSF components will be put together in an adjustable fixture, aligned with the help of lasers. Each major assembly, mid-body, forward fuselage, and wings will be completed in its own mobile tool, which will then roll into place for final assembly. Again, with the help of lasers, the components will be precisely aligned, mated and fastened together. Even at the start of manufacturing, Lockheed Martin expects to perform final assembly from major sub-assemblies to weight-on-wheels in five days. Eventually, this task should be accomplished in under 20 hours.

The JSF airframe, therefore, presents a combination of revolutionary and conventional features, inside and out. Increasingly, though, tactical fighters do not depend on speed on agility. Rather, they are platforms that do two things: gather information and drop weapons.

Large metal forgings, joined by longitudinal ribs, form the carry-through structure between the F-35's wings. The structure is open at the bottom so that the engine can be removed for maintenance. Lockheed Martin

CHAPTER 4
CYBERFIGHTER

A simple simulator had been set up in a suite at the Washington Sheraton hotel, and Gene Adam—acknowledged industry leader in the design of fighter cockpits—was briefing me in his notorious rapid-fire style on the future design and technology of the pilot's office.

The workload of modern air combat was too high for a single pilot, Adam explained, unless information could be arranged logically and intuitively. The way to do that—what Adam called "Big Picture"—was to turn the entire instrument panel into a single uninterrupted screen, capable of displaying a high-definition map, "threat circles" around hostile radars and missiles, and the location and identity of targets and friendliest. Windows in the picture could show infra-red or radar images for target identification.

Gone from the cockpit was the head-up display (HUD). The pilot needed to be cued on to targets outside the relatively narrow cone that was bounded by the HUD's field of view. Instead, the pilot would have what Adam called "a HUD on the head," a helmet-mounted display or HMD, which would be a primary

It was a pretty good description of the JSF cockpit, and Adam backed it up with a dizzying array of overhead slides, because there was no PowerPoint in 1983. Neither did Adam or anyone else have a clue how Big Picture might be made to work. Simulator designers were working on interactive computer-generated displays with something like the level of fidelity that it needed, but they took rooms full of computers to drive them. You could get a back-projection TV about the size of Adam's screen, but it was the size of a piano. Active-matrix liquid crystal displays were laboratory curiosities.

But, Adam observed, those were engineering problems and therefore, in theory, had solutions. Anyway, he said,

high-definition TV would come, and people wouldn't stare at muddy 525-line pictures forever, meaning people would want bigger screens. They wouldn't be CRTs because those wouldn't fit in the living room. Eventually, there would be big-screen flat-panel displays that would hang on the wall, and that would provide the technology for Big Picture.

Did I mention this was 1983?

The JSF is intended to be the most automated fighter aircraft ever built. "The autopilot is intended to operate throughout the mission," U.K. JSF program manager Ivor Evans remarked in mid-2004. On the way to the target, the automatic flight management system will steer the aircraft around and between enemy radars to minimize its signature, while computers generate a list of targets and assign priorities to them. "The idea is that the pilot will paddle-off the autopilot at the last minute, perhaps two miles and ten seconds away from weapon release, then roll away and return to the autopilot mode," Evans said.

This may make the pilot feel like the passenger, but it is probably essential; in today's complex operational environment, with military targets concealed among civilian vehicle traffic or among buildings occupied by non-combatants, a solo pilot—and there is no such thing as a two-seat JSF—has no time to worry about throttle settings, fuel flows and the status of the airplane, unless something goes wrong. "Aviation technology has evolved to the point where the pilot is largely a monitor for the systems," comments one USAF officer. "On a B-2 mission, the pilots take off, go to sleep, wake up and play cards, and consent to weapon release when they get over the target, and they never see the weapon hit. One guy had to reboot his computer [in operations over Iraq]. I think they gave him an air force medal."

Boeing JSF cockpit shows what can be achieved with large-format displays. One side of the screen is devoted to a large moving map, big enough to show a lot of detail without becoming hopelessly cluttered. On the left-hand side, the screen is broken into four windows, including stores management and an IR image, which are still as large as many fighter displays today.
Boeing

Mock-up of Raytheon's candidate radar for the JSF; the Northrop Grumman radar for the F-35 will be similar. The radar antenna is physically fixed and angled backward to reduce its RCS. It is actually a backplane that provides power, cooling, and connections to more than 1,000 tiny radar modules, each with a transmitter, receiver, and pre-amplifier. Bill Sweetman

The JSF pilot, however, will have a better view than B-2 crews—who have only a radar picture of the ground ahead of the airplane. The fighter will have an outstanding set of sensors and displays, so that the pilot can indeed focus on threats and targets.

The JSF's primary sensor is the Northrop Grumman APG-81 radar, a much improved and less costly descendant of the F-22's APG-77. In fact, Northrop Grumman JSF radar technology is already being incorporated in a new-generation radar for the F-22 and in the APG-80 radar for the F-16 Block 60.

The JSF radar has what is called an active electronically scanned array (AESA). Instead of a mechanically steered antenna that moves to track and search for targets, an AESA comprises a fixed planar structure carrying more than 1,000 "transmit-receive modules," each of them a tiny solid-state radar. By firing the modules in different sequences, the radar's computers can change the direction, shape, and intensity of the radar beam instantly.

A report in late 2001 by the Pentagon's Defense Science Board credits AESA radars with "10-30 times more net radar capability" versus mechanically scanned systems. One unique advantage of an AESA is that its design reduces radio-frequency (RF) losses in the radar chain. An AESA can offer several times greater sensitivity than a conventional radar, partly because the receiver is coupled almost directly to an amplifier in each module. As a result, there is very little opportunity for interference or noise to enter the signal before it is amplified, resulting in a very clean signal to the processor.

APG-81 specifics are still classified, but it has been stated that the Raytheon APG-79, under development for the Super Hornet and based on Raytheon's JSF radar technology, can track targets at ranges in excess of 100 nautical miles, almost twice the range of some of today's radars.

The AESA does not have to waste energy on sky that has already been found clear of targets and can concentrate on tracking targets that have already been detected. "Track quality throughout the entire field of regard of this radar is better than the weapon-quality track-while-scan volumes of current weapons," comments a USAF pilot.

AESA offers new capabilities in terms of detecting small targets. One example is "track before detect." An AESA detection threshold can be set at a level that is low enough to pick up false alarms as well as genuine targets. But when the radar encounters a suspicious return, the beam can immediately dwell on the target and confirm it if it is genuine. Returns that exceed the threshold, but cannot be confirmed can still be matched from scan to scan, and if they turn out to be targets, the radar already has track data on them.

The APG-81 will also offer new capabilities against surface targets. Its synthetic aperture radar (SAR) mode will provide photographic-quality images of ground targets at long range and in any weather; Lockheed Martin charts even show SAR images of tire tracks. The SAR picture is expected to be good enough to classify vehicles and tell the difference between targets and simple decoys. By operating in two modes, SAR and ground moving target indication (GMTI), and switching between them almost instantly, the radar should be able to superimpose GMTI tracks on the SAR picture. This is useful because SAR and GMTI are like Jack Sprat and his wife—SAR cannot see targets that move, and GMTI can't see targets that don't move.

The AESA is important to stealth in part because no known stealth aircraft has been built or even proposed with a mechanically scanned radar. The first advantage is reduced RCS. A mechanically driven antenna has a complex shape and is difficult to shroud. The APG-81 array is installed with a slight upwards tilt which deflects the head-on main-lobe reflection upwards and away from any likely receiver. There is still backscatter from the edges of the radar array, which is masked by the use of radar absorbent material (RAM) on the perimeter of the array.

V-shaped sapphire window covers the electro-optical targeting system (EOTS) under the F-35's nose. It provides the EOTS sensor with a near-180 degree field of regard in azimuth and more than that in elevation. Lockheed Martin

If AESA technology has one "killer application" on stealth aircraft, it is low probability of intercept (LPI). AESA greatly expands the number of LPI techniques that can be used to ensure that a stealth platform does not betray its position and identity through radar emissions.

The agility of the radar makes it possible to reduce peak power adaptively, as the target gets closer, the radar power can be decreased rapidly to a point where an intercept receiver cannot detect it. An AESA radar can search simultaneously with multiple beams. Because each beam searches only a small sector, it dwells longer on a given spot and can therefore achieve the same probability of detection with less power.

Given sufficient processing horsepower, an AESA radar can confuse an interception system by varying almost every characteristic of the signal, apart from its angle of arrival, from one pulse integration to the next. For example, it can change its pulse width, beam width, scan rate, and pulse-repetition frequency (PRF), all of which are essential identifying characteristics for interception systems.

An AESA can also do things that are not part of a radar's normal repertoire. Because of its low noise, it is a very sensitive receiver, if not a particularly broad-band one. It also has a very high peak power in the megawatt range, and can transmit a very narrow, intense pencil beam; it has been suggested that the capability would allow an AESA to not only jam radars, but even interfere

with land-line communications links by beaming intense power into connection nodes. In 2000, Raytheon JSF team leader Dr. Peter Pao remarked that the AESA was "much more than a radar . . . It detects and jams enemy radars. It's hard to tell where EW ends and radar begins, and we believe the boundary will disappear in ten years."

The F-35's other forward-looking sensor is the electro-optical targeting system (EOTS), a high-performance, all-digital infra-red system using an advanced, cooled detector array operating in the mid-infrared band. Installed behind a faceted sapphire window, which maintains the airplane's stealth characteristics without allowing IR energy to reach the sensor, the mechanically steered EOTS includes a BAe Systems laser rangefinder. In clear weather, the EOTS can detect and acquire targets from medium altitudes, 20–25,000 feet, and typical slant ranges and pin down their exact location without any radar emissions. It can also detect airborne targets at long range, acting as an infra-red search and track (IRST) system, and will be valuable for visually identifying targets beyond the range of unaided vision.

Northrop Grumman provides the other element of the JSF's electro-optical sensor system: the distributed aperture system (DAS). This comprises six identical, fixed, solid-state infra-red cameras, each covering a 60-degree field of view, using staring mega-pixel-class detectors provided by CMC Electronics. They provide complete day and night spherical coverage around the airplane, with the

The pylon-mounted, full-scale F-35 model outside the avionics integration laboratory in Fort Worth provides a spatially accurate mount for F-35 antennas and allows the systems to be tested in free space. Lockheed Martin

equivalent of 20:40 vision, and with some ability to penetrate smoke and obscurants.

The DAS image will be projected on the visor of the pilot's helmet-mounted display. The JSF pilot will have unlimited night vision, even in very low light conditions (under clouds, for instance) with the additional cues provided by infra-red imagery. For example, other aircraft and moving ground targets are normally warmer than the background and show up better in the IR spectrum than on night-vision goggles. The pilot will also be able to look down "through the floor"—an advantage not only for targeting and situational awareness but for landing the STOVL airplane, whether by day or at night. The only disadvantage is that the through-the-floor view can be initially nauseating.

The helmet-mounted display (HMD) will be a key part of the JSF cockpit, enabling the pilot to stay "head-out" while still having access to flight and target information. An HMD comprises an image generator, a projection system in front of the pilot's eyes, and a tracking system in the cockpit that measures the pilot's look angle and constantly adjusts the projected image so that the picture is always accurately superimposed on the outside world. Time-lag can be worse than nauseating.

The HMD has many uses. If one of the sensors detects a potential target or threat, an arrow on the HMD can tell the pilot where to look for it, saving valuable time in acquiring the object. If the pilot sees or identifies a hostile aircraft, the HMD can pass the pilot's sight-line to a missile seeker, even outside the radar's gimbal limits. The missile seeker can slew to acquire the target and it can, in turn, display its own lock-on on the HMD, confirming that what the pilot sees is what the missile is about to shoot. If the pilot sees a possible target on the ground, the HMD can immediately slew the EOTS on to it, while the sight-line, combined with a digital terrain map and GPS position, allows the onboard computers to determine its exact location. The pilot identifies the target with EOTS imagery, swings around and releases a GPS-guided weapon.

The Lockheed Martin team is working with two leading suppliers—BAe Systems and Vision Systems International, the latter jointly owned by Israel's Elbit and Collins' Kaiser division—to develop alternative HMDs. The challenge is to pack a high-quality optical display system into a helmet that is comfortable and safe for ejection. One specific problem: comfort is hard to reconcile with the need for the helmet to be stable on the pilot's head to keep the pilot's eye aligned with the vision system. Most suppliers agree, too, that the helmet shell needs to be individually fitted to the pilot's head but that the electronics need to remain attached to the airplane. The display unit can be clipped to the helmet, but this complicates efforts to get the weight and balance right.

Reliability and stability will be crucial because the HMD will have to be certificated as the primary flying instrument on the JSF. In particular, it will be the pilot's guidance system for carrier landings; a fact that came as a surprise to a U.S. Navy officer on the F/A-18 program as late as mid-2004. Super Hornet pilots disengage their HMDs on approach and rely on the HUD; rigidly mounted to the airplane, it provides an accurate and consistent flight-path reference.

The HMD replaces the head-up display found on today's fighters. The HUD, essential as it has been, has been a bugbear for cockpit designers, because it requires a large optical chain that precludes placing a display screen at the top center of the instrument panel. With the HUD gone, and using toughened versions of commercial flat-screen displays, the cockpit designers have been able to fill the entire upper panel with a single screen, 20 inches wide by 8 inches high. (Although it operates as one unit, it comprises two 8x10 screens for the sake of redundancy.) The screen is supplied by Kaiser and uses projection technology, which provides greater brightness and contrast than a conventional liquid-crystal display screen with a backlight.

The most likely display format will be a high-resolution digital map, with windows that open as necessary to display IR and radar imagery. Threats detected by the Lockheed Martin/BAe Systems electronic surveillance measures (ESM) system will be displayed on the map, surrounded by circles that indicate their detection range against the stealthy fighter circles that will get larger as the fighter gets beam-on to the threat, smaller as it moves into a nose-on position. With the airplane flying a largely automatic track, the pilot will be using a cursor control more than the throttle and stick.

Even the throttle and stick will command computers rather than being directly connected to the controls; the throttle, essentially, will command acceleration and computers will determine how much power to supply.

The STOVL version places the greatest demands on the integrated flight and propulsion control system. A basic demand is that JSF must be easier to fly and land than the nervous Harrier. Transition into jet-borne flight will be automatic; once the lift-fan is at full power and the aft nozzle is vertical, the functions of the controls will change. Forward and aft movement of the stick will control vertical acceleration. In fact, at this point, the stick has traded jobs with the throttle and controls the engine, not the aerodynamic surfaces. Left or right stick movements will cause the airplane to move sideways, the throttle will command fore-and-aft acceleration, and the rudder pedals will control attitude, not direction, causing the airplane to rotate around its vertical axis.

Like the F-22, the JSF will carry a high-bandwidth, low-probability-of-intercept data-link, which will allow each aircraft in a formation to use and display sensor data from any of the other aircraft. Tactically, this opens up interesting options: one aircraft, for example, can act as a mini-AWACS for the group, using its radar to track targets, while the others can fire and guide AMRAAMs in radar silence. Alternatively, the operator need not all fit all the aircraft in a fleet with a complete avionics suite, reducing costs; or a JSF could be launched with an equipment failure that would normally keep it on the ground, improving availability.

An overarching challenge in the development of the JSF avionics is to ensure that the system can stay abreast of technology. This problem—known as diminishing manufacturing sources (DMS)—has been a serious issue on the B-2 and F-22. Long development cycles have meant that the basic electronic chips around which some systems were designed are no longer in production. Moreover, the industry does not even make components that look like that any more, has not done so for decades, and has no interest in production runs measured in hundreds at best. The answer is to make the systems flexible and based on common

Equipped with JSF radar, EOTS, and other sensors, Northrop Grumman's veteran BAC One-Eleven test aircraft (it has also supported the F-22 and F-16 programs) continues to be used for inflight evaluations of the fighter's new avionics.
Lockheed Martin

A helmet-mounted display (HMD) module is clipped to the pilot's helmet. On the F-35, the HMD will replace today's head-up display, freeing up the space at the top of the instrument panel. In conjunction with the six IR arrays in the Distributed Aperture System (DAS) the HMD will also allow the pilot to see in the dark in all directions, even through the airframe. Boeing

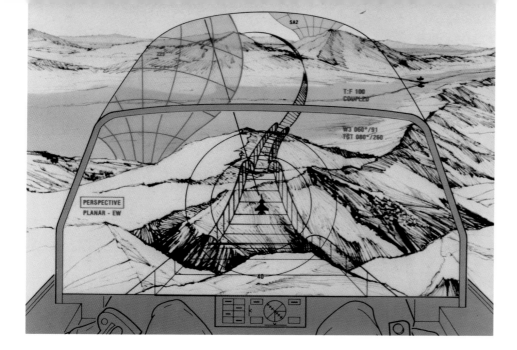

Gene Adam's visionary "Big Picture" concept, devised in the early 1980s, envisaged the entire panel as an interactive display combining stored data, sensed data and imagery, together with the suppression of the HUD in favor of a HMD.
McDonnell Douglas

The basic armament of the JSF comprises two 2,000-pound JDAM guided bombs on the outside of the weapons bay, plus a pair of AIM-120 AMRAAM missiles attached to the inner weapon-bay doors. Stores are ejected by rams driven by high-pressure air, rather than the pyrotechnics used today.
Bill Sweetman

software standards, a so-called "open architecture," so that hardware can change without affecting performance.

The F-35 will carry a wide range of weapons, reflecting both old and new technology, and to a great extent showing that the airplane is, primarily, a bomber.

The first air-to-surface guided weapon on the F-35 when it enters service will be the Boeing joint direct attack munition, a 2,000-pound or 1,000-pound bomb fitted with a simple tail guidance kit, comprising a GPS receiver and an inertial measurement unit (IMU) and steerable tail surfaces. JDAM is often called a GPS-guided weapon, which is a little bit of a misnomer because the IMU is the primary guidance sensor. In fact, when the concept that led to JDAM was conceived in the mid-1980s, it was inertial-only.

Immediately before release, the weapon is programmed with its predicted trajectory to the target. The IMU measures its actual movements and corrects for errors caused by different windspeeds at different altitudes, wobble after release, and other factors; the GPS provides a periodic position check and is particularly effective at eliminating along-track errors. Even if GPS is jammed, JDAM does not go ballistic, it will just be less accurate.

JDAM's tactical advantage is that it is immune to weather and does not require the launch airplane to designate the target so several can be released at once and the airplane can take evasive action. It is also more accurate than anyone expected. At the

start of the JDAM project, the Pentagon expected to develop a follow-on version with a high-precision seeker, but the existing weapon has demonstrated a circular error probability of under 16 feet, compared with the 40-plus feet in the specification. That means that half the weapons released will hit with 16 feet of the aim-point.

This has had several consequences. Because JDAM is so accurate, the Pentagon has realized that, rather than developing a seeker for the weapon, it makes more sense, to reduce the target location error (TLE), the difference between the programmed impact point and the target's actual position. High-resolution SAR and the laser rangefinder in the EOTS both help to reduce TLE.

A more accurate weapon can also kill a target with a smaller warhead so that a single airplane can carry more weapons and there is less risk of collateral damage. In the invasion of Iraq, in fact, some targets were attacked with concrete-filled bombs, reducing collateral damage to zero. The original JDAM was produced in two versions: the 1,000 pound GBU-32 and 2,000-pound GBU-31, but the Pentagon has accelerated production of a modified tail-kit for the GBU-38, based on the 500-pound Mk82 bomb.

Boeing was awarded a contract in 2003 to start development of the even smaller GBU-39 small diameter bomb (SDB), a 250-pound weapon with a folding, diamond-shape wing, which give it a glide range measured in tens of miles, and lattice-shaped folding fins unashamedly copied from the Russians. Specifically designed to allow stealth airplanes to carry more weapons internally, the SDB will be carried on a special four-bomb rack that fits in the F-22 and JSF, allowing them to carry eight bombs

internally rather than two. The goal of the SDB program is to double the number of kills per sortie against 85 percent of targets.

The guide to coordinate the concept of JDAM has been adapted to other weapons. The Navy will arm the F-35C with the AGM-154A and AGM-154C Joint Stand-Off Weapon, the largest internally-carried weapon on the airplane. The A model, operational since 1999, dispenses BLU-97 blast/fragmentation/incendiary sub-munitions, and is primarily intended to destroy air defense systems; the C model has a precision guidance system with a terminal seeker. The USAF will employ the Lockheed Martin wind corrected munition dispenser (WCMD), a guided version of a versatile canister which can release guided or unguided submunitions or even specialized munitions that shower carbon fibers on to power lines and switching stations.

Another advantage of JDAM is that it is cheap. Boeing's JDAM plant, located in St. Charles on the Missouri river flood-plain, is at the centre of a revolution in air-to-surface munitions. When the JDAM project started in 1992, Air Force program managers set what was then considered a very challenging unit cost goal: $40,000 in 1992 values for a complete kit to modify an existing 900 kg Mk84 bomb into a guided weapon. The 2002 price was around $20,000, or well under half the goal and a small fraction of the price of any previous guided weapon. Laser-guided bombs typically cost around $100,000.

The success of the JDAM project in beating its cost target is immensely important, because it makes it reasonable to project a future in which all air-launched weapons will be guided. In Afghanistan in 2001, 10,000 out of 18,000 air-launched munitions used in the operation were precision-guided. According to General Ed Eberhardt, commander of USAF Space Command, half those precision weapons—5,000 in all—were JDAMs.

Theater commander General Tommy Franks contrasted the Enduring Freedom strikes with Desert Storm, in which some 9 percent of the weapons used were guided. "In Desert Storm, we had 3,000 sorties per day. In Enduring Freedom, we had 200 sorties, but they hit the same number of targets that we hit with 3,000 a day in Desert Storm. Then, we used ten airframes to a target; now, we assign two targets to an aircraft." While other factors were in play

for example, Afghanistan's air defenses are almost entirely destroyed; the difference is nevertheless dramatic. In Iraq in 2003, more than two-thirds of the bombs dropped were guided. By the summer of that year, with Iraqi operations under way, the JDAM plant had been expanded and was building towards a peak rate of 2,800 guidance kits per month.

The JDAM's low cost reflects can be traced to the program's launch. The USAF imposed a minimum of basic requirements: a 13 m CEP, compatibility with aircraft targeting systems, a guaranteed 20-year storage lifetime, and a $40,000 maximum cost. Most standard military specifications (Mil Specs) for components and materials were avoided.

The assembly line reflects the principles of lean production. Sub-assemblies such as fins, tail-cones, and guidance systems are delivered to the Boeing plant in containers, which are placed directly on roller racks beside the assembly stations. Each assembly worker has a signal light to indicate when the supply of parts is running low; when the light is yellow, more parts are delivered to the roller racks and empty containers are removed. Assisted lift devices are used for components weighing more than 40 pounds; the hydraulic devices respond to the operator's hand movements.

Handling and processing are minimized. For example, the JDAM ship and store containers are first delivered to the company that produces the weapon's body strakes. The company loads the strakes into the containers before they reach Boeing, and they are not touched again until the complete weapon is ready to be assembled and used in the field. The tail-kits themselves are packed in foam-plastic blocks which are wrapped in a plastic film and vacuum-sealed.

The actual assembly work, however, is performed by hand. This makes the line very flexible, and able to switch almost instantly between different versions of the bomb, which have different-sized fins and tail-cones but are assembled in the same way.

The basic JDAM is being steadily improved to reduce costs and to avoid problems caused by obsolescent components. Changes are grouped in annual blocks. One important change

One option for JDAM is a simple folding wing that can be attached to the bomb in place of body strakes. It does not require any changes to the guidance hardware and gives the bomb a stand-off range of several miles. The USAF is acquiring a similar wing-kit for its dispenser weapons. U.S. Air Force

JDAM in a test flight aboard a Boeing F-15E. The weapon has proven easy to integrate and its accuracy largely depends on the accuracy of the target location; JSF's advanced radar and EOTS will provide the best possible target data, making JDAM a near-precision weapon. Boeing

is the replacement of the Honeywell ring-laser gyro (RLG) IMU with a new IMU based on micro-electromechanical systems (MEMS) technology, which took place in the 2003-2004 production block. From the user's viewpoint, however, the bombs are identical

As AESA and SAR enter service, TLE and weapon accuracy have reached the point where a terminal seeker is required to do any better; the good news is that because of the weapon's accuracy, the seeker only needs to scan a small area for the target. The U.S. Navy has put Boeing

under contract to develop the Hornet autonomous real-time targeting (HART) system for the Block 2 F/A-18E/F, which has the APG-79 AESA radar. HART uses the AESA to acquire a high-resolution SAR image of the target, which is transformed into an image template for an infra-red seeker attached to a modified GBU-38 500-pound JDAM.

HART weapons should be operational on the F/A-18E/F at the end of 2007, and a similar system could easily be developed for the F-35. That is likely to happen, since later versions of the GBU-39 small diameter bomb are expected

AMRAAM—the first widely-used air-to-air missile with an active radar seeker—has ushered in a revolution in air combat. With AMRAAM, the fighter no longer needs to illuminate the target all the way from launch to impact; it merely needs to track the target (while it can still search for others) until the AMRAAM's miniature radar locks on to it. U.S. Air Force

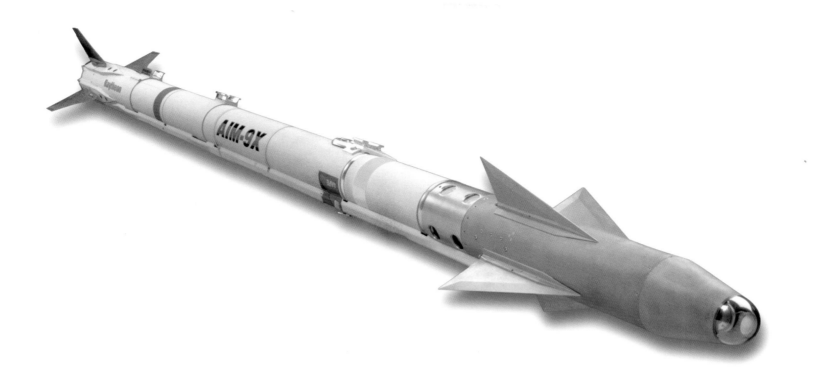

to feature a seeker and data-link for precision attacks against moving targets.

Virtually all the air-to-ground weapons that the JSF will carry internally in stealth mode are JDAM-related. The only exceptions are 500-pound GBU-12 laser-guided bombs, which remain part of the baseline. Their main advantage is in "sniper" missions where precision is essential and where target information may be provided by ground troops with hand-held designators or by an orbiting UAV.

The primary air-to-air armament of the JSF, in U.S. service, is a pair of Raytheon AIM-120 advanced medium-range air-to-air missiles (AMRAAMs), carried on launchers built into the inboard weapon bay doors. The details of this installation are significant. Two AMRAAMs constitute a defensive load, not armament for a fighter sweep, and there is no provision to carry more AAMs internally, replacing the bombs. AMRAAM itself, without a short-range AAM to back it up, is mainly a defensive weapon. The idea seems to be that a formation of JSFs could take a shot-of-opportunity against a non-stealthy interceptor that had identified itself by using its radar using LPI radar modes, ESM, or EOTS to provide the missile with initial and mid-course guidance.

Also, the weapons' location results in a rather limited field of regard for their seekers, bounded on one side by the weapons bay door and above by the fighter's lower fuselage. Essentially, any missile launched from the weapon-bay door is going to be fired as AMRAAM normally is fired, in lock-on after launch (LOAL) mode. This will also apply to the MBDA advanced short range AAM (ASRAAM), which will be the standard AAM for U.K. JSFs.

LOAL is the only option for a long-range engagement but has a problem at short ranges, where the target aspect may change dramatically and unpredictably, and by the time the missile clears the airframe the target may not be where it was and something else may be in that location. LOAL, remarks one fighter pilot, "is like putting a pit bull in a gunny sack, shaking him up and letting him out; he's going to bite the first thing he sees." The missile location implies that the JSF is not intended to get into dogfights at close ranges, as long as it is operating in a stealthy configuration.

The JSF will take advantage of continuous improvements to the AMRAAM. The current production version in 2003 was the AIM-120C-5, which combined clipped wings, to fit the internal bays of the F-22 and F-35, with a longer motor, made possible by redesigning the tail control section. It is being followed by the AIM-120C-7, also known as the Pre-Planned Product Improvement Phase 3 version. The C-7 started its firing trials in 2003 and is due to become operational in 2005 with the Navy's F/A-18E/F Super Hornet as its first platform. The C-7 will be the initial AMRAAM standard for the F-22.

Thrust vectoring makes the AIM-9X Sidewinder agile at short ranges, and smaller wings and a more streamlined nose make it faster and give it a longer range than earlier AIM-9s. However, the warhead and motor are drawn from large stocks of older AIM-9 variants. Raytheon

AIM-9X in tests from an F-15. If a target is detected by radar, and under clear conditions, the AIM-9X seeker can lock-on to a target that is well beyond visual range. The target pilot has no idea that he is under attack, because the missile has no radar emissions. U.S. Air Force

The primary change in the C-7 missile, relative to the AIM-120C-5, is new processing hardware, which has made it possible to improve the weapon's resistance to electronic countermeasures (ECM). The guidance and ECCM software has been re-hosted and is now based on C++ programming language, making it easier to upgrade; a new software release, due in 2006, can be installed on any C-7 missile and will further improve ECCM. The new processors form a stack of "hockey-puck" modules rather than a single long circuit board, releasing six valuable inches of space for later enhancements.

In December 2003, the Pentagon awarded a contract to Raytheon covering development of the AIM-120D, previously known as the P3I Phase 4 missile. It is due to be fielded in late 2007. Raytheon will replace the current inertial measurement unit (IMU) with a combined global positioning system (GPS), and install a new two-way data-link. The GPS/IMU will reduce alignment errors and, combined with new software, will make the missile more effective at long range.

The new data-link and GPS allow the missile to report its own position to the launch platform; this increases the confidence that the missile is guiding on to the correct target, which is particularly important in a high off-bore-sight (HOBS) engagement where the missile is outside the fighter's radar coverage and is being cued by an off-board asset. The data-link will make it possible for a fighter to guide a missile launched from another aircraft or from the ground.

What the AIM-120D does not have is a new motor, even though the missile is out-ranged by both the Vympel R-77 and the MBDA Meteor. A Raytheon executive says that the missile's basic kinematics "continue to be looked at." The purpose of the extended motor on the C-5 was "to get to the same range faster," rather than to increase range. "You can have a 100-mile range missile," the executive notes, "but if you can't get an identification you can't shoot. It's better to ID at a certain range, and then get there faster."

Although the F-35 does not carry a short-range AAM in stealth mode, it does carry the oldest fighter weapon—a gun. It might seem logical to ask why. Gun technology has not changed fundamentally since the introduction of the General Electric M61 Gatling cannon in the 1950s, and the percentage of gun kills has declined since Vietnam, when the poor reliability of AAMs showed that the U.S. services' elimination of the gun had been premature.

While the effectiveness of the gun has remained roughly constant, AAMs have been greatly improved, and this improvement has been tracked in a declining percentage of air-to-air kills attributed to guns. The most dramatic shift took place with the introduction of the AIM-9L Sidewinder and similar AAMs in the late 1970s, which offered a much wider launch zone around the target than earlier tail-chase weapons. In the Arab-Israeli war of 1973, guns accounted for 70 percent of Israeli kills. In 1982, over the Bekaa Valley in Lebanon, 93 percent of the kills were made with missiles; in the Falklands war in the same year, there were no air-to-air gun kills.

With the advent of improved short-range AAMs coupled with helmet-mounted displays, the need for the gun would seem to have declined even further. In a classic within-visual-range (WVR) engagement, the advantage belongs to the aircraft that can turn and accelerate more quickly to place the target within the envelope of its missiles. With modern AAMs and HMDs, the launch zone around the shooter is expanded to almost a complete hemisphere while missile range is greater, increasing the number of firing opportunities. As a result, the chance of being attacked without warning from an unexpected direction—the most dangerous kind of attack—has increased. It follows that getting anywhere remotely within gun range of a target is something to be avoided.

On the other hand, gun advocates argue that the weapon still has its uses: in a multi-target engagement when ranges and speeds steadily reduce until the opponent is in gun range, for slow targets like UAVs and helicopters, and as a form of intimidation against hijacked aircraft where a gun could be used to damage an airplane and give its passengers some chance of survival. If a fighter was scrambled to intercept a light aircraft, potentially carrying a chemical, biological, or radiological weapon, the gun might be the best way to destroy it without dispersing its payload in the air.

But the fact is that Vietnam inoculated an entire generation of U.S. fighter pilots against any future desire to remove the gun from fighter aircraft and that generation is in command today. Guns were specified without question on the 1970s generation of fighters and with rather more controversy on the F-22, requirements for which were drafted in the 1980s, and on the JSF 10 years later.

The complicating issues on the JSF were weight and the attitude of the navy, which has always regarded JSF as a bomber and saw no pressing need for the gun. Weight was a problem for the STOVL airplane: from the outset, it was clear that weight would be critical, whether for Lockheed Martin or Boeing, and the STOVL version could not afford 450-plus pounds for a gun that would be carried on every mission, needed or not. Another factor was that the program office wanted a weapon with a longer effective range than the 20 mm M61.

Both teams initially proposed a development of the 27 mm Mauser BK gun, a revolver cannon developed in Germany for the Tornado and Typhoon. The weapon was to be co-developed by Mauser, which invented the revolver cannon in the 1940s and ATK, which had acquired the former McDonnell Douglas gun business from Boeing. However, the ATK weapon proved more expensive than expected, and the USAF, which already shoots 20 mm M61s, 30 mm GAU-8/As, and 25 mm GAU-12/U guns on AC-130 gunships, had no desire to add a fourth medium-caliber round to its logistics chain.

The competition was re-opened, and GD was selected as the JSF gun integrator in September 2002. The new gun will be a variant of the 25 mm GAU-12/U Equalizer, the five-barrel Gatling that is currently used on the AV-8B

Harrier II, and the AC-130U. The individual rounds are not quite as accurate as today's 27 mm round, but the gun puts more of them on target, with a rate of fire of 4,100 shots/min and the kill probability should therefore be reached. The 25 mm gun is already available with a wide range of ammunition, including multi-purpose types.

GD is responsible for developing the internal gun and feed system for the F-35A and a podded weapon for the F-35B and F-35C. The internal weapon weighs 461 pounds, including its feed system and 180 rounds of ammunition. The podded weapon will be self-contained, including its 220-round ammunition supply, and the helical feed system coils around the gun itself will be mounted on the centerline pylon without interfering with the weapon bay doors.

Imagery from the AIM-9X seeker, split seconds from impact on a QF-4 target. Imaging seekers are extremely hard to decoy because they can be programmed to distinguish between the characteristic shape of an airplane and the diffuse shape of a decoy flare. Raytheon

A Raytheon AGM-154 joint standoff weapon (JSOW) about to hit the center of a target complex. Such accuracy is making it possible to reduce the size of weapons, destroying the target while reducing damage around it. Raytheon

The F-35 has seven external stations for other weapons: four heavy wing stations, a 1,000-pound centerline station (displaced by the gun pod on the F-35B and F-35C), and SRAAM stations on the wingtips of the F-35A and F-35B and under the outer wing of the F-35C. Under the SDD program, the airplane will be fully cleared with 500-pound GBU-12 Paveway II laser-guided bombs, 500-pound unguided bombs, and 425 U.S. gallons fuel tanks, to be used mainly for ferry flights.

Another standard weapon for external carriage is the Raytheon AIM-9X Sidewinder. The AIM-9X was conceived in the early 1990s, after it became abundantly clear that Russia's highly agile Vympel R-73 SRAAM outclassed anything in the West. After a series of classified and white-world demonstration programs and a drawn-out Pentagon decision process, the Naval Air Systems Command awarded GM-Hughes Missile Systems Company a $169 million contract in December 1996 to develop the AIM-9X. Hughes has since been acquired by Raytheon.

The selection of the AIM-9X, the most conservative of several proposed missiles, surprised those who had expected that a larger motor would be essential to match the kinematics of the R-73, but the winning design had two points in its favor. One was cost: it uses motors and warheads from the AIM-9s that are in the current inventory. The seeker, tracker, and the Stirling-cycle cryogenic system are derived from existing hardware. The thrust-vectoring system is derived from ATK's work on Evolved Sea Sparrow, and draws on low-cost technology developed for the joint direct attack munition. The result is a missile with a target average cost of $264,000 in then-year dollars, a very significant advantage when the U.S. services plan to buy 10,000 rounds.

The other point in favor of the AIM-9X design was that while its kinematic performance was not as good as that of its rivals, or the much bigger R-73, it is good enough. The AIM-9X, Raytheon claims, will beat the R-73 because of two crucial and often overlooked factors. The first is that, although we talk about the "within visual range" engagement, imaging IR missiles will reliably lock-on to targets at ranges where even the most eagle-eyed fighter pilot cannot consistently detect them. The second is the difference between the Russian helmet-mounted sights and the new U.S. helmet-mounted displays.

In JHMCS, but not in the Russian sights, target information can flow up to the display. Tests have shown that an HMD-cued pilot will consistently see and identify another aircraft at a greater range than an unaided pilot. This makes it possible to exploit the full capability of the AIM-9X imaging IR seeker, including the fact that it has a longer range than the simpler non-imaging seeker of the R-73.

A Lockheed Martin AGM-158A JASSM cruise missile drops from an F-16, just before deploying its wings and fins. The jet-powered JASSM has a range of more than 200 miles and has proven accurate enough to hit a specific door or window in the target building. Unlike today's cruise missiles, it is inexpensive enough to be produced and used in large numbers. Lockheed Martin

The AIM-9X, says one source, "is a BVR missile." Its low drag and efficient flight control system compensate for the small motor, and its seeker reaches well beyond visual range—up to 12 nautical miles—and can be cued directly by radar or the EOTS. It gives the pilot the option of a passive attack well beyond the lethal envelope of today's AIM-9. Full-rate production deliveries started in 2003, and the missile was declared operational in November. Raytheon is developing a LOAL mode to allow the AIM-9X to be used at extreme range or to engage targets behind the launch aircraft.

JSF is intended to carry two longer-range air-to-surface missiles: the U.S. Lockheed Martin AGM-158 joint air-to-surface standoff weapon (JASSM) and the Anglo-French MBDA Storm Shadow.

JASSM is a 2,250-pound, turbojet-powered cruise missile with a range of more than 200 nautical miles and a 1,000-pound warhead. GPS navigates it to the vicinity of the target. An IR sensor in the nose images the target and the missile's computer compares it to a visual template loaded before the mission and based on reconnaissance images. Its accuracy is phenomenal: JASSM can be reliably guided to hit a specific window or door on a target building, and its multi-purpose warhead is effective against hard targets. Small size, shape, a non-emitting guidance system, and the selective use of RAM make JASSM stealthy.

JASSM was developed along the same low-cost lines as JDAM, and has emerged with an under-$500,000-per-unit price tag, less than half the cost of earlier cruise missiles. The missile's composite airframe is constructed using techniques borrowed from boat builders and is being produced in a new plant in Troy, Alabama. A total staff of 100 people is expected to deliver more than 40 missiles per month. The weapon was declared operational, on the B-52, in October 2003 and full-rate production was authorized in 2004.

Development of the AGM-158B JASSM extended range (JASSM-ER) started under a contract awarded in February 2004. Production missiles should be available in 2008. Externally identical to the AGM-158A, the longer range missile has a larger fuel load and a more powerful and efficient Williams F107 engine, giving it a range of more than 400 miles.

Storm Shadow was used operationally in 2003, in support of the invasion of Iraq. Slightly larger than JASSM, weighing some 2,860 pounds, it uses GPS and inertial guidance in the cruise, backed up by a system that compares the terrain below the missile with a stored map. An IR terminal seeker and target-recognition system are used in the final attack. It has a BAe Systems Broach warhead, which fires in two stages: a forward-facing precursor charge blows a hole in a hardened target and the second stage passes through and detonates.

The JSF, therefore, will have a highly effective range of weapons and sensors. But the same weapons and sensors can be easily fitted to other airplanes and indeed, this is already happening. Will JSF be revolutionary enough to justify its existence?

CHAPTER 5
GOING GLOBAL

In mid-2004, I had a conversation with a French air force officer, a manager for a major weapons program. We exchanged comments on the JSF for a few minutes, and then the officer asked a question. Did I think that the purpose of the JSF was to destroy the European Union?

I was lost for words. My immediate reaction was that the Frenchman needed a tinfoil hat, that anti-American paranoia had gotten the best of him. But I had to admit that from the standpoint of a European fighter professional, JSF could be seen as a direct and intentional threat to Europe's collaboration on high technology military equipment.

Two regular characters in Steven Spielberg's *Animaniacs* cartoon series were the mutant laboratory mice Pinky and the Brain. In every episode, the Brain's response to Pinky's query about the night's plans was constant. "The same thing we do every night, Pinky—we're going to take over the world."

That, in essence, was the JSF plan for the fighter business, and it still could succeed.

The roots of United States dominance of the fighter business extend to the 1950s, when Cold War military aid programs directed hundreds of aircraft, many of them F-86 Sabres, rebuilding air forces of Western Europe. Later in the decade, though, France and Britain, with the most active aircraft industries in the region, started to discuss deals under which other European nations would not simply buy their airplanes, but collaborate in their development, reducing the drain on their import-export balance and building up their home industries.

The French and British plans were scuppered by Lockheed, with a mixture of advanced technology, industrial competence, hard-edged salesmanship, and (in some cases) good old-fashioned bribery. Germany, the Netherlands, Belgium, Denmark, Italy, and Norway contributed to the development of the F-104G StarFighter, a substantially modified, export-only version of a fighter that had enjoyed only limited success with the USAF. More than 1,100 of the high-performance and occasionally dangerous airplanes, the Luftwaffe, it was said, defined an optimist as a StarFighter pilot who quit smoking, were assembled in Germany.

In the early 1970s, the Pentagon, under the leadership of James Schlesinger, emerged from its preoccupation with Vietnam and turned to strengthening its ties to European allies. The USAF, which had spent the 1960s pursuing plans for expensive and specialized fighters with little export appeal, was persuaded to make room for a less costly, more versatile air combat fighter (ACF) which was specifically conceived as an exportable airplane that could replace the F-104G.

The result was the General Dynamics F-16, which utterly defeated a scattered and disorganized group of European competitors in 1975, winning export sales to a key group of customers: the Netherlands, Belgium, Norway, and Denmark. The fighter went on to achieve export successes worldwide. Then, the F/A-18 Hornet rolled up other major export customers: Australia, Canada, and Spain.

The European response was disorganized and slow. There was no direct response to the F-16 and F/A-18, although Dassault successfully sold its Mirage 2000 in a number of countries. In the mid-1980s, France launched its Rafale program and Britain, Germany, Italy, and Spain started development of what became the EuroFighter Typhoon, but both projects ran into post-Cold War reassessments and budget cutbacks and development dragged on through the

The USAF may be committed to JSF, but its priority is the supersonic-cruise F/A-22. The addition of the small diameter bomb will improve the F/A-22's capability in the strike role, and a delta-winged bomber version—the FB-22—is being considered. U.S. Air Force

Success of the F-35B STOVL fighter is crucial to the United Kingdom, because its new carriers—Prince of Wales *and* Queen Elizabeth—*are being built without catapults. The new ships will have turbines for high speed and diesel engines for cruise, with electric final drive.* Thales

1990s. Meanwhile, the F-16 and F/A-18 continued to dominate world markets and, in the process, provided valuable support to government-nurtured defense industries around the world.

The goal of the JSF was to continue that dominance and expand it, in several ways. First, JSF combined the home markets that had launched the F-16 and F/A-18, plus the marines' 600 aircraft, so it started with economies of scale that the Europeans could not match. Initially, the Pentagon planned to buy more than 3,000 JSFs for domestic use, which was three times more than the combined home markets for the Rafale and Typhoon. Secondly, the cost targets—to be achieved by a combination of high production rates, lean production and new technology—would make the fighter more than competitive with European rivals. Third, the JSF would build on the United States' proven ability to integrate other national industries into its major programs, and the large numbers would make industrial participation even more attractive. Finally, the JSF offered a range of technologies, led by stealth, and advanced, built-in sensors the rest of the world was not ready to match. It was hard to see that anyone would want to buy anything else, unless they needed airplanes before the JSF was ready or they had been embargoed by the United States.

By mid-2004, this plan was on the surface succeeding. International partnership agreements had been signed. The largest and firmest of these is the United Kingdom's commitment to replace its joint-service Harrier STOVL force with the F-35B. The four original F-16 nations, the Netherlands, Belgium, Norway, and Denmark, have also committed money to JSF, entitling them to bid for contracts and to place representatives in the program office. Canada and Australia have provisionally selected the JSF to replace their large F/A-18 fleets and have also paid their entry fees, as have Turkey, Italy and Israel. Singapore has also signed on to the program.

However, it is important to remember that none of these countries has signed or been offered a binding contract to buy JSFs and the around-$40 million price tag is a goal, not a fixed value.

Out of all the partners, the most committed is the United Kingdom, due to a series of decisions that followed the contract award to Lockheed Martin. In 2002-2003, the British Ministry of Defence (MoD) reorganized its plans for its Harrier force. At the time, the fleet comprised a mixture of shipboard Royal Navy Harrier FA.2s, based on the original Harrier airframe but equipped with a radar and AMRAAMs, and a larger number of RAF Harrier GR.7s based on the Anglo-U.S. Harrier II. The navy's aircraft were based on

the three small aircraft carriers delivered in the 1970s, which were themselves reaching the end of their useful life. Under a 1998 defense review, the United Kingdom had decided to build two new carriers.

By 2002, the MoD had started the CVF carrier program, with an in-service date of 2012. The ships would be much larger than the old Invincible class, with the ability to carry 24–30 fighters, plus airborne early warning aircraft and Merlin antisubmarine helicopters. U.K. defense leaders also decided that the fighters would form a joint RAF/navy force that would supersede both the RAF and RN Harriers. Meanwhile, the existing aircraft would be blended into a new joint force Harrier (JHF) based on the GR.7 and an upgraded, more powerful GR.9. The FA.2 would be retired by 2006.

One final and largely irrevocable decision remained to be taken in the summer of 2002. The new CVFs looked like

50,000-ton ships at almost 1,000 feet long, smaller than the U.S. Navy's *Nimitz* class, but close to the size of *USS Forrestal*, the first super-carrier. They would certainly be big enough to launch and recover the CV version of JSF. It was a difficult decision; the CV version offered more range, but experience had shown that, particularly for a mixed land-based and sea-based force, STOVL imposed a smaller training burden. The final decision, announced in September 2002, was that the carriers would operate STOVL aircraft.

Thales, United Kingdom, a division of a French company, and BAe Systems will collaborate to build the new carriers, which will be named *HMS Queen Elizabeth* and *Prince of Wales*. The design has changed since the contract was awarded, but the ships will carry a bow ski-jump, boosting the performance of the STOVL aircraft, and will not have

any catapults or arrestor gear. Without a STOVL aircraft, the carriers are large and expensive paperweights, and the F-35B is the only STOVL fighter in sight.

STOVL has remained a controversial issue, to some extent, in the United States. It is part of a dilemma: people are willing to accept that the United States has an army, a navy, and an air force; and even that the navy has its own air force, navy aviation, and army. But does the navy's army need its own air force?

The marines have enjoyed enough support in Congress to fend off this question for many years, but economic realities have already persuaded the navy to push for greater integration of marine and navy air units. One result is that the navy's JSF requirement is not completely solid. Official program documents still put the navy JSF requirement at 480 aircraft, alongside 609 short take-off, vertical landing F-35B aircraft for the Marine Corps. However, a navy plan issued in early 2002 called for closer integration between navy and marine tactical air power and a cut in navy/marine JSF orders to a total of 680 aircraft. How these would be divided between F-35Cs and F-35Bs has not been disclosed. Another factor of uncertainty is that, of all the JSF customers announced to date, the navy is the only one that has a modern fighter, with an AESA and advanced cockpit in production, in the form of the Super Hornet. If the JSF is late, the navy may well extend Super Hornet production.

In an effort to boost confidence in the STOVL version, USAF leaders announced in early 2004 that the service would buy some F-35Bs, with the aim of improving its ability to operate from rudimentary airfields, close to ground troops. Some statements gave the impression that the F-35Bs would represent additional orders, because the JSF would replace the A-10 ground attack aircraft, which has proven very useful in Afghanistan and Iraq, as well as F-16s and F-117s. However, that is not quite accurate. The USAF always planned to retire the A-10, and in fact the decision to buy F-35Bs probably results in a cut in total numbers, because the STOVL airplane is more expensive than the F-35A. Again, official documents still list a USAF requirement for 1,763 JSFs, but a recent briefing merely said that the air force would buy "more than 1,000" airplanes.

Underlying these issues, in mid-2004, was the realization that there are serious problems in the JSF program. International participation is not working as well as it did on the F-16. A largely secret debate in the United States is threatening the program's long-term health, because some people would like to block export customers' access to stealth technology. The most immediate problem, however, is weight, followed by money.

If the STOVL JSF was built and delivered to its summer-2004 design standard it would be incapable of performing its design mission because the design is 3,300 pounds overweight, which is more than 10 percent more than the operating empty weight estimate in Lockheed Martin's winning proposal. Some of the reasons have been discussed earlier in the book; they include a complex internal layout and, probably, the difficulty of designing large doors which operate in high-speed, hot, noisy airflows, must seal near-perfectly after take-off to maintain stealth characteristics, and must open with 100 percent reliability on landing. But what many commentators missed was the impact of the weight growth.

Weight gain on most airplanes is not the end of the world. There's usually some margin to increase the take-off weight and landing weight, so the payload remains the same and the range is only marginally affected. Other factors may offset a weight increase: the engine may beat its fuel-consumption target or drag may be better than expected.

That is not the case with a STOVL airplane, because landing weight is directly tied to engine thrust. If the airplane is overweight, that excess must be matched by an increase in thrust or it comes directly out of the fuel and weapon load; the "bring-back" load, with which the airplane can land.

Bring-back comprises a safe amount of reserve fuel, enough to allow for missed landing attempts, more at night than in daytime, plus any weapons that were not used in the mission. The second element is more important than it used to be: combat pilots used to drop bombs on anything that looked like a target if the primary target was unavailable, and in the last resort, dollar-a-pound dumb bombs could be dumped in the sea. Today, random bombing is forbidden by rules of engagement and expensive guided weapons cannot be tossed away lightly. Bring-back is

crucial; in fact, the chief rationale for the navy's F/A-18E/F program was that the old C/D version had run out of bring-back due to added equipment.

The math is quite simple: the design gross weight of the F-35B is around 30,700 pounds, bringing the weight to 34,000 pounds with the overrun. The design vertical thrust of the fan-boosted propulsion system is 39,600 pound. With a modest 5 percent thrust margin on vertical landing, this leaves only 3,750 pounds for reserve fuel, weapons, and a pilot. The ability to land vertically with fuel reserves, two 1,000 pound GBU-32 JDAMs, and two AIM-120s is a key performance parameter (KPP) in the JSF requirement but is clearly not attainable unless weight can be reduced.

By mid-2004, a "STOVL weight attack team" or SWAT had been formed to look at every aspect of the program. The challenge is to avoid shortening the airframe life by substituting lighter components, or increasing costs by using exotic materials, or sacrificing commonality. The team is reluctant to pull more power from the engine; neither the

F135 nor F136 has been tested, and the risk is that boosting output will consume temperature and stress margins. Reports suggest that the team is hoping to eliminate 2,400 pounds of the overrun while demonstrating that fuel reserves can be safely reduced.

The JSF schedule has been slipped. Critical design review (CDR)—the most important early milestone in the plan—was due in April 2004 but will not take place until November 2005. The first F-35A, aircraft A-1, will fly in the summer of 2006 rather than late 2005. However, the first three aircraft will be spread over a longer period than originally planned. JSF B-1, a STOVL F-35B, will fly almost a year later than the first aircraft, in mid-2007, a full year behind schedule.

Moreover, under the revised plan, the A-1 and B-1 aircraft will be delivered to an interim standard, without the weight-saving improvements to be incorporated in later aircraft. Pentagon and Lockheed Martin program managers stated in May 2004 that these two aircraft would "enable valuable ground and flight testing," but it is likely that they

While the USAF focuses on the F/A-22, which is too expensive for export customers, and the not-yet-available JSF, Sweden has started to make inroads in the world market with the tiny but capable Gripen. Its secret: networking technology that is more advanced than any other fighter in service, which allows a flight of Gripens to fight as one airplane. JAS

Britain, Germany, Italy, and Spain have invested tens of billions in the EuroFighter Typhoon and are desperate for export markets. Eurofighter salesmen are keen to point out that export customers will get the most advanced Typhoon available—not a sanitized export version. Eurofighter

will not make a full contribution to the flight-test effort. The same applied to the first three F-22s, which were not delivered to the full structural strength specification.

The third aircraft, and the first JSF to incorporate weight-saving modifications—C-1, the first carrier-based F-35C—will not fly until the late summer of 2008. This is 16 to 18 months behind the first F-35B and at least 18 months behind the original schedule. The completion of Block 1 flight testing, which delivers a basic aircraft armed with AIM-120s and JDAMs slips by the same amount, was ,moved to the autumn of 2010.

The new schedule is rather more concurrent than the previous plan. Although the first flights of critical test aircraft, the first STOVL JSF and the first weight-reduced aircraft, are 12 to 18 months late, approval for low-rate initial production (LRIP) slips by under a year and is set for early 2007, before either of those aircraft have flown.

The final LRIP schedule had not been released by mid-June 2004, but outline schedules have been discussed in public. Now, initial operational capability (IOC) is targeted for early 2012 with the U.S. Marine Corps, about two years late. The USAF IOC slips to 2013, almost two years later than original scheduled and at the same time as the navy F-35C. According to one Lockheed Martin document, the United Kingdom's IOC is "to be determined" but no earlier than the USAF and navy.

A large number of F-35s will be on order before tests are completed. It is now likely that the first low-rate production batch of ten aircraft (six CTOL and four STOVL) will be fully

funded in 2007 and delivered two years later, in 2009. Thereafter, production accelerates quickly: 22 aircraft delivered in 2010, 54 in 2011, 91 in 2012, and 120 in 2013. The sixth and final LRIP batch of 168 aircraft will be delivered in 2014. If these numbers hold, LRIP will include 465 aircraft, which is 50 percent more than the total planned F-22 production run.

Almost a quarter of the USMC's aircraft will be produced during LRIP (even based on the 609 aircraft that the Marines nominally plan today), because the marines need aircraft early to meet their 2012 IOC. In terms of airframe development, this makes the STOVL version "the long pole in the tent." In system-manager jargon, this refers to the longest sequence of tasks in the basic schedule.

Along with the delay comes a sharp increase in systems development and demonstration (SDD) costs. "Additional design maturation" will cost an extra $7.5 billion across the life of the program and "aircraft configuration updates" are expected to add $7.8 billion to the cost of SDD, according to the Pentagon's Selected Acquisition reports, released in April 2004.

Meanwhile, there are rumblings of discontent from international partners. The most vocal critics have been in the Netherlands and Norway, where companies such as Stork and electronic-warfare manufacturer Terma did very well from the F-16 program. It has to be said that some of the criticism is unjustified because the partner governments and industries should have known that the rules for JSF were not the same as the rules for the F-16.

On the F-16 and similar programs, contracts were assigned to international partners as part of the deal under which the airplanes were sold. On the JSF, program managers made it clear from the outset that costs were paramount. Every subcontract would be awarded on the basis of cost and competitiveness; even after winning, suppliers would have to reduce their costs at a stipulated rate and any contract could be recompeted. JSF leaders argued that the massive rewards of a 5,000-airplane program made the business far more valuable than a similar contract covering 620 Typhoons or 300 Rafales, and that they did not need to be generous.

Another aspect of the JSF environment was that there were three main contractors on the program from the start: Lockheed Martin, Northrop Grumman, and BAe Systems, all with payrolls to meet and mouths to feed. They were very different from the companies that launched the F-16, as a result of 1990s defense consolidation. Lockheed Martin and Northrop Grumman had extensive experience in infrared systems, Northrop Grumman made radars and BAe Systems (among many other things) produces flight control systems, HMDs, and electronic warfare systems. The program office could argue until it was blue in the face that the selection of subcontractors would be fair, and that the prime contractors' corporate cousins would be assessed on the same basis as all others; but the art to winning a contract is often that of knowing how many resources to commit to which campaign in the first place, and that is where a company like BAe's Information and EW Systems unit had an advantage. Not only was it part of BAe, but it had previously been part of Lockheed Martin.

Not even BAe Systems is entirely happy. "JSF was . . . a massive disappointment for us," remarked Chairman Sir Richard Evans in early 2004. "That took us out in the U.K. from the common aircraft business and we will live to regret it. It is no good when you have signed up and paid your cheque over then trying to go back to negotiate the release of technology. It is absolutely not the way to do it. There will probably be two or three major updates throughout the large program, and we know that one of those updates will be undertaken by Lockheed . . . and not here in the U.K."

Efforts by competitors to chip away at JSF's position by offering more work packages in the old-fashioned way

have not been successful so far. EuroFighter has mooted the idea that export customers could take a major role in developing the Tranche 3 version of Typhoon, intended as a multi-role aircraft with an AESA and other new features, but the plan has been stalled because the EuroFighter partners themselves have been unable to pin down the configuration of Tranche 2, let alone Tranche 3. Opposition has been confined to grumbling.

A much bigger issue—the elephant in the living room— is access to stealth technology. Stealth was a deadly secret when it was first conceived. If you visited an office anywhere near a stealth program, and did not have the specific clearance that said that you had access to it, your escort kept you in sight at all times and carried a bell or a flashing light and buzzer to alert the staff to the leper in their midst. I was in Seattle in 1998 and took a tour of the F-22 flying laboratory, a 757 with the F-22's radome and sensors. When I asked a question and pointed to a feature on the radome, the Boeing engineer almost stiff-armed my hand away. The radome was "touch-classified;" people without clearances were not permitted to lay a finger on it.

It seemed odd that the Pentagon was even thinking about opening such sensitive and valuable technology to foreign customers, particularly in view of the fact that it

The U.S. Navy is solidly committed to JSF—but if it does not work, or if it is late, the service is also very happy with the F/A-18E/F Super Hornet, which is still in production. It is not stealthy and does not have the JSF's range, but it does have advanced avionics and a two-seat option. Boeing

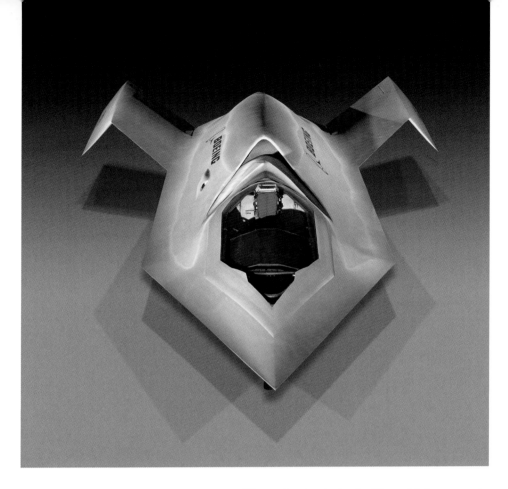

Making JSF a tri-service aircraft within a fixed budget, and at low risk, meant turning down promising technologies like the next generation of stealth, represented by Boeing's Bird of Prey *demonstrator. Developed secretly in the mid-1990s and declassified in 2002, the* Bird of Prey *was designed for both ultra-low RCS—in the small-bug class—and visual stealth.* Boeing

was still spending hundreds of millions of dollars a year to protect it on still-secure programs like the F-22 and B-2. It has been estimated that the special access program (SAP) security measures attached to such projects add 15 to 20 percent to their cost. It was odder still that a straight answer to this obvious question was hard to come by. Strangest of all was that none of the potential customers seems to have asked the question at all.

During the demonstration phase of the program, one common answer to questions about LO exports was that the problem was a matter of details that could be resolved at a later date. This was and is debatable. The U.S. taxpayer has not spent triple-digit billions on stealth technology because it is a nice-to-have add-on that complements the other attributes of a combat aircraft. LO drives the design of a military aircraft in the same way as it drives the design of a submarine. If the goal is real stealth, 30 to 50 decibels under the 1m2 reference target, everything from details as small as canopy latches to training and support is subordinate.

Stealth requirements are also likely to have changed since the JSF program started. In particular, the USAF is likely to have upgraded its LO requirements because of the continuing threat from advanced surface-to-air missiles and the reduction in the planned fleet of F-22s, the aircraft which were originally expected to provide cover for the JSF.

The United States—and still has—three basic options for exporting the JSF, one of which is unworkable.

The first is to deliver identical, stealthy aircraft to the United States and export customers. The challenge is to do so without compromising essential technology. Although a major goal in the development of JSF is to create LO systems, such as coatings and seals, which require less maintenance, it is unlikely to be reduced to zero; flight-line personnel will physically handle, remove, and replace LO materials as a matter of course.

Materials are not the whole story. JSF simulations show cockpit displays which project "threat circles" around hostile radars. These are driven by computer software hosted on the aircraft and on the desk-top mission planning system, which can compute the detection range of a radar against the JSF in real time. The threat circles are determined by two sets of data: a detailed model of the fighter's radar cross-section (RCS) at every relevant frequency and aspect angle, and a database that reflects the latest assessments of potentially hostile radar systems. Both sets of data are extremely sensitive and valuable. If an adversary obtained this software, it would dramatically improve his ability to tailor and organize defenses against the JSF, and the damage would be practically irreparable.

The second basic solution was to deliver a sanitized export JSF from which the most sensitive materials and technologies are eliminated. Some early discussion of the LO export problem focused on "modular stealth" and pointed in this direction. But stealth is not a matter of reducing RCS and hoping for the best. It is vital to model RCS, accurately, reliably, and in detail, and to use that model as the basis for mission planning, diagnostic tools (is the aircraft stealthy enough today, against this particular threat array?), and even maintenance. Degraded stealth without such a database is not stealth at all. In this case, JSF would not represent any advance over a new-generation F-16 because its stealth could not be relied upon in combat.

The third approach is an export JSF using less sensitive materials, but still reflecting a disciplined approach to LO. There are some basic problems with this concept. First, it involves duplicate research and development, because LO is very influenced by details. It would demand another complete program of RCS engineering, including design and tests of full-scale models, and both JSF programs have used very detailed, sophisticated models and flight tests. Changes would not be confined to coatings and a few edge structures; JSF is full of specially designed apertures and antennas.

In service, a "less-stealthy" JSF would require differences in maintenance training and support. Mission-planning software would be different and would have to be separately supported and updated throughout the development process. Coalition commanders would not be able to assign different nations' JSFs to the same missions and targets.

The problem would be exacerbated by the fact that the most effective LO technologies are the most sensitive, so the LO differences are not likely to be trivial. Export customers will have to sell their taxpayers on the idea that they are paying $50 million apiece for aircraft which are, all other things being equal, more likely to be shot down than the aircraft flown by the United States.

The design of a non-stealthy or less-stealthy JSF raises other questions. If it is not stealthy, should it have an active jamming system, including a towed decoy? Will it need short-range AAMs for the close air combats that will no longer be avoided? Any such steps will degrade commonality and make the aircraft more directly comparable to the F-16 Block 60 or Typhoon.

It took two years after the start of the program for an answer to this question to emerge, in a post-9/11 world where allies were less important than they had been at the start of JSF. The long delay seems to have reflected a controversy among Pentagon leaders, stretched out by a complex and opaque decision-making system covering stealth.

Early in 1999, Lockheed Martin's deputy JSF program manager, Harry Blot, suggested that the DoD was moving towards a common LO standard for all JSFs under pressure from the theater commanders-in-chief, who were anxious to avoid the problems of operating two or more different standards of aircraft. Little more was heard about it. By early 2002, program vice-president Tom Burbage would say only that the company "was under contract to design a single configuration," adding little to previous statements that JSF exports would be in accordance with national disclosure rules. In 2003, a JSF program official said that the export versions "would look the same," implying that materials under the surface might be different. Another source says that "all JSFs will have stealth features" but will not confirm that all of them will be identical in LO performance.

The problem was that the JSF program office did not have the authority to resolve the problem. The release of

An unmanned combat air vehicle (UCAV) could emerge as an alternative for some JSF missions by 2015. The Boeing X-45A, flown in 2002, has evolved into the much larger joint unmanned combat aircraft system (J-UCAS), with JSF-like offensive weapon load and greater range. Boeing

information concerning LO systems is controlled directly by the Secretary of Defense, who is advised in these areas by two Pentagon organizations. The National Disclosure Policy Committee (NDPC) is an inter-agency group, including the services and intelligence agencies, which makes recommendations to the Secretary of Defense concerning release of all classified or controlled information. However, there is a parallel and separate system covering stealth technology, centered on the LO/Counter LO executive committee (LO/CLO Excom). The Excom comprises representatives from the central LO offices in each service, the Signature Technology Office in the USAF Research Laboratory, for example, and is chaired by the under-secretary of defense for acquisition, technology, and logistics.

The Excom's executive secretary is the DoD's Pentagon-wide director of special programs, who also heads the Special Access Program oversight committee (SAPOC). This organization oversees stealth programs and other classified projects, including "black" programs which are so secret that their existence and purpose are classified.

The Excom's recommendations, therefore, reflect not only the need to protect technology used in stealth aircraft which have been publicly disclosed, but also secret research programs. Consequently, they may be driven by factors unknown to anybody involved in JSF.

The LO/CLO Excom was certainly pivotal in establishing ground rules for the United Kingdom's participation in JSF

and other stealth programs. The United Kingdom and United States have secretly collaborated on stealth for many years; there was a U.K. exchange pilot on the F-117 program before its existence was disclosed, and there is no reason not to assume that the United Kingdom would have access to a fully stealthy JSF. However, this does not mean that BAe Systems would have such access: the F-117 deal was strictly a government-to-government arrangement.

One source close to the JSF program says that the Pentagon's theatre commanders-in-chief (CINCs) have consistently advocated a single JSF configuration, because multiple levels of LO would complicate joint operations, but that the LO community itself, covering JSF, F-22, and other programs has opposed this view fearing technology compromise. "The commanders in the field want coalition allies to have highly capable aircraft; it's the lower level people who don't want to share the technology," he says.

Finally, late in 2003, Lockheed Martin was awarded a $600 million supplemental contract covering the development of an "international partner version" for the JSF, including "a version of the JSF . . . that is as common as possible to the U.S. air system within the National Disclosure policy."

The use of less sensitive materials on export JSFs is likely to be accompanied by a range of new anti-tamper (AT) measures, an area that has received increasing attention since 9/11. According to the FY2003 and subsequent Pentagon budgets, the air force is responsible for developing AT technology for electronic hardware, including transmit/receive modules for electronically scanned arrays, software, and radar absorbent material (RAM). Technical support is provided by Sandia National Laboratories in Albuquerque, New Mexico, which is operated by a division of Lockheed Martin.

AT technology for electronic hardware and software exists in the commercial world. One way to protect hardware is to encase components in a material that cannot be removed without destroying the component. Software anti-tamper measures are used to protect confidential data stored on notebook computers or personal digital assistants (PDAs). Lockheed Martin, in fact, is a major client for PDADefense, which develops such systems. Essentially, the software detects unauthorized access attempts and in some

Breakthrough supersonic technology could result in a new supersonic bomber by the mid-2010s. Unlike JSF, it could sustain high sortie rates even if bases close to the conflict were closed by threats of terrorism or by political pressure.
Northrop Grumman

cases destroys data with a "logic bomb" if too many attempts are made. AT technology is part of a multi-layer security system that partitions software and controls access on a need-to-know basis.

Jeff Hughes, directing the USAF laboratories' anti-tamper efforts, says that protecting materials is "a tough area; it's an ongoing investigation as to how much [protection] is good enough. You need reasonable protection, balanced against implementing the weapon." The goal, he says, is to "slow or prevent" exploitation. For example, there may be parts of the JSF that will not need to be accessed in normal operation, and they may be covered by rules analogous to warnings on consumer electronics that the warranty is void if the user opens the case. "Access detection and denial" is identified as a specific area of effort for the USAF/Sandia project.

Another source suggests that export customers would not necessarily need the ability to repair complex LO materials. The JSF program goal is to have two-level maintenance and to make LO systems so durable that they seldom require maintenance unless they suffer impact damage. "Now, whether you're going to export the capability of repairing a leading edge, I don't know," he says. "You might ship it back and change it for a spare part." One problem with this approach, though, is that no known LO program has achieved its maintainability targets yet.

A former program official, though, stresses that final decisions about export configurations have not been taken. Export JSF deliveries—beyond the United Kingdom—will not start for at least ten years. "What's the world going to look like ten years from now? Nobody knows. The real answer is that as we mature our capabilities, we develop our partners and their ability to control, manage, and do the work."

Even so, the idea that export JSFs may be less stealth and less survivable than U.S. aircraft is hardly a selling point and is already encouraging potential competitors overseas. Moreover, there are also competitors emerging for JSF funding within the United States.

Technically, other Pentagon projects don't compete with JSF, but as a practical matter they do; in any given year, there is only so much money to go around.

One such competitor is the unmanned combat air vehicle (UCAV). Now gathering pace, the joint unmanned combat air system (J-UCAS) is aimed at developing an unmanned strike-reconnaissance aircraft with a JSF-like weapon load (two 2,000-pound JDAMs or 8-12 SDBs) and a range of more than 1,000 miles. Air force and navy versions are being developed. While there is still a good deal of skepticism about the project in the field, it will be interesting to watch the first J-UCAS make a carrier approach and landing, bringing back 4,000 pounds of bombs; program managers are confident that they will have early operational vehicles not long after 2010.

JSF has enormous momentum—thousands of jobs already hang on the program—and would be very hard to stop even at this stage, but it has some way to go before the name "ultimate fighter" has truly been earned.
Lockheed Martin.

J-UCAS won't cover the entire JSF mission spectrum. But for the U.S. Navy, for instance, it covers much of the JSF's unique missions. For the navy, first-day, LO, long-range precision strike is what the JSF does and the F/A-18E/F Super Hornet does not, and the J-UCAS will do that mission well, if it works.

J-UCAS could also exploit the kind of ultra-stealth technology featured in Boeing's *Bird of Prey* demonstrator, a secret airplane tested in 2002 but declassified in 2002. Quite clearly, *Bird of Prey*, named after a Klingon craft in *Star Trek*, is aimed at developing technology that would allow stealth aircraft to survive unescorted in clear daylight with an ultra-low RCS, a shape that does not generate strong shadows and counter-shading on the airframe.

Experience in Iraq has even started the USAF thinking about new bombers, rather than fighters, an amazing turnaround for a service that is led and dominated by fighter pilots. It was not that USAF fighters could not operate effectively over Iraq; the problem is that neighboring states such as Turkey refused to allow U.S. forces to operate from their bases, fearing counter-attacks from terrorists. Such "anti-access" threats forced fighters to make long sorties with multiple inflight refuelings, leading to crew fatigue and potentially deadly errors.

In early 2004, the USAF started talking openly about new long-range strike systems, possibly starting with an FB-22, a radically modified version of the F/A-22, or with a supersonic-cruise airplane based on current research into low-sonic-boom jets. Rather than pushing the IOC for such aircraft out to 2037, the USAF is talking about bringing such an aircraft into service before 2020.

Another issue is whether the JSF is really what is needed for the conflicts of the 2012 and beyond. One unexamined issue is the value of first-day stealth; a concept based on the 1991 Gulf war, where a formidable air defense network was lobotomized on the first night of operations and functioned afterwards at a fraction of its efficiency. More recently, particularly in Kosovo, the pattern has been different. Defenders have relied less on fixed,

integrated systems, and more on informal, hard-to-target networks of improvised communications links and observers. Unpredictable and unmapped threats are still a factor days and weeks into a conflict at a point where JSF is expected to be carrying external weapons to deal with many, small targets. A JSF in that condition is not stealthy, but lacks an active jammer and towed decoy, two survivability features that have proven very valuable for non-stealthy fighters.

JSF is a single-seater; a two-seat version exists only on paper. In the early 1990s, the need for the two-seat fighter, usually regarded as a training device, seemed to be diminishing. Today, though, the two-place airplane seems to be making a comeback for a number of reasons. One of these is the vast amount of imagery and data accessible to the crew: SAR images, video from advanced infra-red sensors, onboard digital maps, reconnaissance images datalinked from UAVs, or even from spacecraft. It may be more than one pilot can handle, even with the highly automated JSF. Another feature of current two-seaters is the AESA: within physical limits, it can act as two radars in one so that the pilot can monitor airborne threats while the weapon system operator (WSO) in the back seat uses the radar in SAR/GMTI mode. Finally, the rules of engagement and weapon release in current conflicts are restrictive: two crew members, working all the available sensors, may be better able to confirm that a target is hostile.

The revival of the two-seat airplane is not a matter of theory. Most Rafales will be two-place airplanes, and so are most of the navy's Block 2 Super Hornets, most of Israel's F-16I fighters and a large proportion of the United Arab Emirates' F-16 Block 60s. The Block 2 F/A-18F has a specially designed aft cockpit dominated by a large-format display screen; so does Sweden's JAS 39D.

Despite increasing costs, a weight problem, and nervous export customers, JSF is a promising program. But, in 2004, the next few years look more than interesting for this very ambitious airplane. Destroying the European Union will just have to wait.

INDEX